370
.971
Gal

BRADFORD WEST GWILLIMBURY P. L.

P9-DOA-214

33528900281755

Pushing the limits : how schools can pre

Aug. 23, 2017

PUSHING THE LIMITS

PUSHING THE LIMITS

How Schools Can Prepare
Our Children Today for the
Challenges of Tomorrow

Kelly Gallagher-Mackay
and Nancy Steinhauer

DOUBLEDAY CANADA

BRADFORD WG PUBLIC LIBRARY
425 HOLLAND ST. W
Bradford ON L3Z 0J2

Copyright © 2017 Kelly Gallagher-Mackay and Nancy Steinhauer

All rights reserved. The use of any part of this publication, reproduced, transmitted in any form or by any means electronic, mechanical, photocopying, recording or otherwise, or stored in a retrieval system without the prior written consent of the publisher—or in the case of photocopying or other reprographic copying, license from the Canadian Copyright Licensing Agency—is an infringement of the copyright law.

Doubleday Canada and colophon are registered trademarks of Penguin Random House Canada Limited

Library and Archives Canada Cataloguing in Publication

Gallagher-Mackay, Kelly, author
Pushing the limits : how schools can prepare our children today for the challenges of tomorrow / Kelly Gallagher-Mackay, Nancy Steinhauer.

Issued in print and electronic formats.
ISBN 978-0-385-68538-2 (bound).—ISBN 978-0-385-68539-9 (epub)

1. Educational change—Canada. I. Steinhauer, Nancy, author
II. Title.

LA412.G343 2017   370.971   C2015-906510-0
C2015-906511-9

Jacket and text design: Five Seventeen
Jacket photos: (blackboard) virtualphoto; (balloon) RubberBall Productions; both Getty Images
Printed and bound in the USA

Published in Canada by Doubleday Canada, a division of Penguin Random House Canada Limited

www.penguinrandomhouse.ca

10 9 8 7 6 5 4 3 2 1

Penguin
Random House
DOUBLEDAY CANADA

NS:
To my father, Paul,
whose advocacy for children still inspires me daily;
and to my son, Samuel,
whose own critique of the education system keeps me
grounded, questioning and searching for answers.

KGM:
To my family, Nuan Qi, Xinke and Sam,
on whom I rely for inspiration, insight and support.

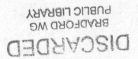
DISCARDED
BRADFORD WG
PUBLIC LIBRARY

"The key to the future of the world is finding the hopeful stories and letting them be known."

—PETE SEEGER

CONTENTS

INTRODUCTION:

GREAT STUDENTS, GREAT SCHOOLS . . . 1

1. BEYOND THE BASICS 11

2. TEACHING CREATIVITY 43

3. SOCIAL-EMOTIONAL LEARNING 69

4. TECHNOLOGY 105

5. SCHOOLS OF CHOICE 141

6 SCHOOLS CAN'T DO IT ALONE 159

7. THE CHILDREN WE SHARE 187

8. IT'S ALL ABOUT THE TEACHER 207

ACKNOWLEDGEMENTS . . . 231

ENDNOTES . . . 235

INDEX . . . 249

GREAT STUDENTS, GREAT SCHOOLS

"The aim of education must be the training of independently acting and thinking individuals who, however, see in the service to the community their highest life problem."

—ALBERT EINSTEIN

"I wouldn't say I'm successful. I'm on the way to being suc-cessful. It's a work in progress," says nineteen-year-old Sakaana Yasotharan, coming out of the first year of her communi-cations degree.

She might be modest, but at home, in the dense, low-income neighbourhood of Jane and Finch in northwest Toronto, Sakaana is aware that she is already an inspiration and a role model. She feels it when she goes to her church, which doubles as a commu-nity hub, and speaks to other young people: "It gives them hope to know there is something past the streets we live in—that there is definitely a better future."

Sakaana was born in Canada to parents who emigrated from Sri Lanka. She has seen talented peers become trapped by drugs, gangs, pregnancies and poverty. But that was not her experience. Her path to success runs straight through the schools that guided her. After being chosen to participate in an enrichment program in middle school, Sakaana sought out a high school that would allow her to remain in a highly academic environment. Encouraged by her parents, she chose to attend an innovative new school with a math and science magnet program—one that would require her to go outside her district. At John Polanyi Collegiate Institute, she was given the opportunity to work on projects that explored what makes schools and neighbourhoods strong. By encouraging her to develop solutions for her own world, her education was strengthened by purpose and context outside the classroom.

According to Sakaana, her school "instilled motivation in kids to have a dream and go after it. If you want to change something—about yourself, your institution, the world—that's why school is important." When a school bolsters students' capacities to dream and their confidence that they can enact change no matter their starting circumstances, it is preparing them for the future. Sakaana is now the informal mentor to a twelve-year-old girl from a Somali family of six kids—helping the girl to set goals and save for university, and sharing the appetite for learning that she developed at John Polanyi.

Colin Walmsley is a recipient of a Rhodes Scholarship, a prestigious prize designed to enable outstanding students—who, according to the Rhodes Trust, "demonstrate a strong propensity to emerge as 'leaders for the world's future'"—to study at the University of Oxford. Colin makes things look easy, from catching a long pass to linking big ideas with everyday experience. But before he was a Rhodes Scholar, Colin was a public school student in Fort Macleod, Alberta, a town of three thousand people just south of Lethbridge—where only three kids went on to university in his graduating year. Despite its mediocre reputation for academics, in his small public high school among the wheat fields he gained confidence and learned to think critically. Through a semester-long project, he and his classmates were asked to renegotiate the world's borders. In science class, they were challenged to critique the tests their teacher gave them. Colin benefited from a series of educators who found the time to show a keen student how he could expand upon what he had learned in a class full of students with very different abilities.

About a third of his class was Mormon, a third Indigenous—mostly from the nearby Piikani and Kainai Nations—and a third, as Colin put it, "the rest of us." For the most part, these three camps remained divided. He witnessed his Mormon classmates taunted for their beliefs, and his Blackfoot peers attacked with racist stereotypes. His high school years offered Colin a close look at inequality and prejudice, and showed him how a school's vision and expectations can serve to enforce or dismantle those barriers.

Early on in Colin's high school experience, after a routine change of principal, students who had been on a path to drop out were redirected, and more and more made it to graduation and beyond. Perhaps educators had previously been reluctant to invest in teenagers who showed up late for class, or even drunk, assuming they were likely to drop out regardless. But with the new administration came a new message. Students sent to the office might be disciplined, but they also had talks about their futures, what they needed to succeed and how to live up to higher standards. The year Colin graduated, the school celebrated ten Indigenous graduates—the most it had ever had.

Colin's teachers empowered him to ask questions and explore his intellectual interests, and showed him how powerful external pressure can be. As he saw his peers survive and even succeed at school as a result of their new administration, he grew increasingly curious about "how people in marginalized communities interact with structures of power"—an interest that grew into concrete research. Now a master's student in public policy and social anthropology, Colin is focusing his research on queer street youth in big cities, and how public policy can make their lives better. His high school was not acclaimed for academics, and yet, perhaps unexpectedly, it *did* ignite his passion for learning and set him on a course to success.

Tiannie Paul and Aaron Prosper are two high-achieving Mi'kmaw youth who graduated from their on-reserve school determined to lead and serve their communities. Tiannie is the first Indigenous student in Cape Breton University's Engineering Transfer Program. When she looks ten years out, she sees her path in environmental engineering positioning her to address chronic infrastructure problems: "In Cape Sable, the water is brown-black. I want to be the person who can fix it—and talk to the elders in Mi'kmaq to make sure we aren't disrespecting their wishes."

Aaron is en route to becoming a doctor—a long-time goal. In grade 11, he contacted the dean of medicine at Dalhousie for advice about getting into medical school. The dean wrote back the same day; apparently, no high school student had ever reached out to him before. Now in the third year of his Bachelor in Medical Sciences degree, when he goes home to Eskasoni, the largest Mi'kmaw community in Nova Scotia, he can sense how much "people are looking forward to the thought that maybe one day we'll have a doctor from our own community treating us."

Like Colin, Aaron and Tiannie attribute their success to lessons more social or emotional than academic. Theirs is a system, says Tiannie, that "pushes us until we get somewhere." The students are expected, and also supported, to succeed. The goal is to unlock every student's full potential, and make all feel valued and capable.

Tiannie and Aaron's schooling started in the late 1990s, just as the Mi'kmaq regained autonomy over their own education system. The thirteen Mi'kmaw communities established Mi'kmaw Kina'matnewey (MK), an education authority responsible for promoting academic excellence and protecting the communities' culture and educational rights. MK has identified identity, community and learning for every generation as central to its students' well-being, and ensures that its schools help students to foster all three. Tiannie's mother nearly dropped out of high school when she became pregnant in her teens, but MK had designed a cohort program to launch adolescent mothers into science careers. Today, Tiannie benefits from support at home and at school. Aaron believes MK has contributed to his own achievement, providing him with a sustaining sense of connection: "MK has really fostered that identity—you are Mi'kmaw no matter where you go, no matter what anybody says. Everything you do is Mi'kmaw." MK's emphasis on community did not merely support him during the stresses of his studies and adolescence, it also gave his studies an urgent, critical edge that shaped his development as a scientist. He is currently engaged in research on the ethics of epigenetics (how genes are shaped by their environment), with a group of researchers who want to track the intergenerational impact of residential schools at the gene level. Aaron is wrestling with how to engage survivors ethically in the study—how to build trust and ensure community benefit from the research.

What do the experiences of Sakaana, Colin, Tiannie and Aaron tell us about how schools can most effectively prepare our students for the future? To meet the demands of an increasingly complex, globalized labour market, all our children must develop their creativity, flexibility and problem-solving abilities like never before. Our world requires they be active, informed citizens and strong communicators who can enact meaningful change. Great schools embrace broad purpose. They build mastery *and* creativity. They support the whole child and in doing so bring in the wider community. Great schools embrace the complications of families, and manage the seemingly unquenchable desire of many parents for choice and personalization in relation to the education of their children in ways that benefit all students. And great schools are supported by strong systems that ensure teachers have the resources, space and inspiration they need to realize the full potential of every student.

Schools are our largest public investment in the future. They are also our largest public investment in childhood. Great schools represent the potential for a more just society and an enriched childhood for every child. They can be engines of universal equality, foundations for strong communities, and vehicles for individual self-definition and advancement. Coming to a common understanding of what our schools *can do* helps to shape and raise expectations, and is a necessary step in making every school great. As parents, educators and citizens, we should expect nothing less.

In researching these great schools, we spoke to a number of teachers, administrators, parents and students. In some instances, where children are referred to by their first names only, their names and identifying features have been changed to protect their privacy.

Within the world of education, it is widely recognized that effective learning builds on the strengths of the learner rather than focusing only on the gaps. Too often, however, conversations about schools focus exclusively on what is missing, overlooking what is there. Without minimizing the significant problems affecting many of our schools today, we do not see the existence of real challenges as a reason for despair. Nancy is a principal with experience that runs the gamut from inner-city to elite private schools, and Kelly is a lawyer, education researcher and public school advocate. We are both parents of school-age children. In our deep engagement with the school system, both of us are convinced that the best place to look for schools that prepare our children to push the limits and navigate the unknown is not in a utopian fantasy, but on the front lines of our current school systems. Schools of the future exist in the here and now, and in this book, we go out and find them.

ONE

BEYOND THE BASICS

"Firstly, there is the conflict between emphasis on factual knowledge and basic skills and the development of attitudes, interests and general abilities. There has never been a decade without critics to lash the elementary school for failure to teach the three R's as effectively as in the golden age to which the particular critic belonged."
— Report of the Royal Commission
on Education in Ontario, *1950*[1]

There is a widespread perception that Canada's schools aren't "sticking to their knitting," that they aren't teaching students the things they need to know. Nowhere is this concern more intensely expressed than in the "math wars" debate that is a common feature of our news cycle. If we are to believe some media commentators, our students are no longer learning the basics. Our schools, we are told, have succumbed to the latest educational fads, focusing on math concepts and creative problem-solving instead of on teaching the core skills every student needs, like the times tables.

The future our students face is unknown, but one of the few certainties is that knowledge of technology and science will be hugely valuable; the stakes for schools to teach math properly are high. But is a renewed and determined focus on the basics indeed the best way forward? Or might an emphasis on real-world applications of mathematic principles be equally important? What tools should students develop now to prepare them for their futures? This chapter will highlight the work done at George Webster Elementary School in east-end Toronto and within Mi'kmaw Kina'matnewey, the Indigenous education authority in Nova Scotia—work done to meld basics-based learning with more complex problem-solving, privileging neither and valuing both, boosting students' results and fostering their longer-term engagement with education in the process. But first, a note about context.

Falling Test Scores—and What They Really Tell Us

Highly respected international test scores released by the Organisation of Economic Co-operation and Development (OECD) reveal that Canadian students have slipped from the top ten economies in math scores and fallen in performance between 2006 and 2015.[2]* Though some argued about the meaning of the rankings (after all, several of the top-performing "economies" were newcomers to the testing program and were cities, not whole countries, which skewed results), their voices were drowned out by more alarmist reactions. In 2013, John Manley, from the (then) Canadian Council of Chief Executives, declared the fall "on the scale of a national emergency," explaining that Canada "needs knowledge workers to really improve our prosperity and build our society."[3] In 2014, the *Edmonton Journal* ran the twenty-six-part series "The Great Canadian Math Debate," with headlines like "Parents demand a return to conventional ways in math" and "This new math is stealing their confidence and their dreams."[4] A year later, the CBC's phone-in program *Cross Country Checkup* asked listeners: "Is there something wrong with how math is being taught?"[5]

The talk of national emergency sent governments and media looking for causes, and a popular narrative emerged: Canadian students were not doing well in math because of a failure of teachers and schools to spend time on the basics. Frustrated

---

* Test scores fell from 532 in 2003 to 516 in 2015. This change is statistically significant. Overall across the OECD, the mean math score fell by ten points in the same period.

mothers of eight-year-olds who didn't know how to multiply publicly shared their stories, and a C.D. Howe report by math professor Anna Stokke told them "faddish" inquiry-based learning was to blame. Stokke insisted direct instruction on basic skills like fraction arithmetic and times table memorization should constitute 80 percent of time spent in math.[6]

Math is a soft target. The anxiety that comes from watching an eight-year-old struggle with the seven times table bleeds easily into a common-sense explanation for declining performance among fifteen-year-olds asked to use math tools to solve problems, interpret the results, and apply them to judgments and decisions about the real world. But the connection misses an important nuance: although math achievement among Canadian students has declined, a variety of measures tells us our students are generally doing quite well with their basic math facts. Where they fall behind those at the very top of international test measures is on questions that require them to apply those skills in novel situations and to unfamiliar problems.[7]

So, for example, on the Programme for International Student Assessment (PISA), a global education survey, 96 percent of Canadian students were able to handle a Level 1 problem that asked them to read a graph tracking music sales and identify what month one band outsold another; but only 39 percent of Canadian students were able to solve a Level 4 problem requiring them to calculate the maximum number of people who could pass through a revolving door in thirty minutes if the door had a two-metre diameter, made four rotations a minute and only allowed two people to enter at a time. In Shanghai, the top-performing jurisdiction, 89 percent of fifteen-year-olds answered the Level 4 questions correctly.

In 2016, half of Ontario grade 6 students failed to meet provincial math standards. However, two-thirds of the Ontario provincial math exam tests students on "thinking and application questions": questions that demand more than just the application of an algorithm, instead requiring multi-step reasoning. Students who can simply do calculations—or basic math—do not meet the standard. A false dichotomy between students *either* learning the basics or having the opportunity to do complex learning in real-world contexts misses the crux of the challenge.

Twenty-First-Century Skills
The United Nations Educational, Scientific and Cultural Organization (UNESCO) was one of the first groups to explicitly address what skills students would need to thrive in the twenty-first century, assembling a blue-ribbon panel of experts from Europe, Asia, Africa and North America to consider the question. Its 1996 report, *Learning: The Treasure Within*, emphasized the importance of education systems that wrestle directly with the key emerging tensions of our times—between the local and the global, tradition and modernity, long-term and short-term goals, competition and equality of opportunity, material and spiritual goals, and the proliferation of information and humans' ability to assimilate it. Faced with the challenge of defining goals that could work across a very broad range of contexts, in both the global north and south, the UNESCO group settled on four pillars all educational systems should adopt: *to know, to do, to live together* and *to be*. These goals pointed well beyond the 3Rs: reading, writing and arithmetic.

In North America, the influential Partnership for 21st Century Skills, a coalition of business and government organizations within which tech companies like Apple and Dell play a significant role, has been campaigning to promote both "the 3Rs *and* the 4Cs": critical thinking, communication, creativity and collaboration. The 4Cs, they argue, need to be incorporated across all traditional subjects. As Helen Soulé, executive director of the Partnership, noted, "Possessing content knowledge is incredibly important, but without the skills to put that knowledge to work through effective communication, creation and innovation, problem-solving, perseverance and flexibility, its value as a pathway to success is significantly diminished."[8]

In Canada, these ideas have been picked up by groups like the Conference Board of Canada. Drawing on interviews with Canadian business leaders, the board compiled a list of "employability skills," which included the basics, such as "using numbers," but prioritized higher-order and interpersonal skills such as managing information, adaptability and teamwork.[9]

And ironically, research conducted by the Canadian Council of Chief Executives at roughly the same time that the organization declared "a national emergency" in relation to declining math scores indicated that the top five skills business leaders look for in potential employees are so-called "soft" skills—people skills, communication skills, problem-solving skills, analytical abilities and leadership skills—echoing the conclusion that students will need more than knowledge of a few key sets of facts.[10] Whatever you call them—twenty-first-century skills, employability skills or higher-order skills—the need to develop them among our students will have profound implications for the schools of the future.

Welcome to George Webster: School of the Future?

At first glance, you would not think of George Webster Elementary School as a school of the future. Located a ten-minute bus ride from the subway in a nondescript part of east Toronto, the school boasts no space-agey design mirroring *Jetsons*-style fantasies. The exterior of this kindergarten-to-grade-5 school is a typical, somewhat gloomy example of 1950s school architecture in yellow brick. You are more likely to see teachers and students working together in conventional classrooms than in immersive technology environments where students spend all day interacting with and through computers. In fact, when Nancy arrived as principal of George Webster in 2008, she was underwhelmed. The school's doors were locked to parents and the community. The windows had bars. On average, students' performance on standardized tests suggested they were a year below grade level, and absenteeism was high.

Upon entering the building, however, she saw a school that ran against stereotypes. Inside, the terrazzo floors gleamed, and the front hall had a park bench casually placed in front of the main office, where a mother and her preschooler were sitting, having a chat. Walking into that front hallway, Nancy was greeted by the chair of the school council and the head caretaker, who were curious to meet the new principal. They stood in front of a notice board with flyers and posters advertising opportunities within the community. A big sign in English, Urdu, Bengali, Tamil and Dari welcomed people to the school and requested that all visitors report to the office. The office sign announced itself in five languages as well.

George Webster hosted a mix of Canadian-born children, immigrants and refugees. Students came from approximately thirty-five different countries and spoke about thirty different languages. When Nancy first arrived at the school, there were quite a few Dari-speaking families from Afghanistan. Over time, the Spanish-speaking population grew, as families arrived from Mexico and Colombia, escaping the political turmoil there. Later, North Korean families arrived, along with families from the Democratic Republic of the Congo, Roma from Croatia and Hungary, and families fleeing Syria.

The students at George Webster live on the downside of an increasingly unequal world. On a school board measure of demographic and socio-economic advantages, George Webster placed in the bottom 10 percent of Toronto schools. In 2008, 75 percent of George Webster students were living in poverty; about half the families survived on thirty thousand dollars or less per year, and another quarter survived on less than fifty thousand dollars. Despite the high level of need, the community had little or no public housing. Instead, families lived in substandard apartments that rented at relatively low prices but were still much more expensive than the subsidized housing at the other end of a sixty-thousand-family waiting list in the city of Toronto—a list on which the average wait for families was well over five years.[11] A few families lived in bungalows, but most students came from the high-density high-rises that could be seen from the playground.

Under the previous principal, George Webster had applied to the Toronto District School Board (TDSB) to become a Model School for Inner Cities, which would endow it with extra funding to provide exemplary programs and supports for its students and community. Becoming a Model School required staff and parents to come together—across significant language and cultural barriers—to make a detailed plan demonstrating how George Webster and the larger community might be transformed academically and socially through the program, and how they might make use of new resources. The endeavour was a success, and in 2007, George Webster was named one of Toronto's first ever Model Schools for Inner Cities.

The Model Schools initiative—the first significant effort to improve inner-city education in Toronto since the forced amalgamation of school boards in 1998—emerged from the 2005 Model Schools for Inner Cities Task Force, made up of educators, academics and politicians. The creation of the task force reflected grassroots efforts to build schools that could respond to child poverty in the vast TDSB—one of North America's largest educational boards, serving over half a million children and youth in 550 schools. The task force wrestled with the question of how best to equip students from diverse and disadvantaged backgrounds to participate fully in an increasingly complex society.[12] It used student-level data about income, family education, immigration status, receipt of social assistance, student mobility and lone-parent structure to create an index of external challenges facing schools; the Model Schools were chosen from the quarter of schools where students faced the most significant challenges. Geographical analysis showed that these schools tended to be clustered in seven distinct neighbourhoods across Toronto, the same ones that came to be called "priority neighbourhoods" by the city because of their concentrated disadvantage, lack of services, and problems like higher crime, shortages of decent housing and poor health outcomes.

The task force envisioned inner-city schools where students would flourish, think critically and understand the perspectives of others, while acquiring the skills and confidence to compete successfully in the outside world. There were five critical steps to realizing that vision: Model Schools would need to be proactive in meeting the social, emotional and physical needs of students; they would embrace their role as "the heart" of their communities; they would evaluate their work; share best practices through local and board-wide networks; and above all, they would adopt innovative teaching and learning methods.

Initially, George Webster split a pool of one million dollars with four other nearby schools. Over time, the number of schools sharing the same amount of funding increased dramatically: by 2015, twenty-two schools shared the million dollars. With continual school board reorganization, it has become more and more difficult to allot distinctive funding for Model Schools.

Sheila Cary-Meagher turned eighty in 2015. She was first elected as a school trustee of the old Toronto Board in 1972, and was one of the coordinators of the task force and a political champion of the Model Schools program. She remembers the battle to get the Model Schools funded in a fiscal environment where there was an overwhelming pressure to treat all schools as if they were the same (while allowing almost unlimited fundraising that primarily benefits wealthier schools). At the heart of the initiative for Sheila was the push to allow teachers to "take responsibility for learning in the classroom" and "challenge the assumptions that poor kids can't learn." With political support and exceptional resources behind them, the staff at George Webster was now well placed to appraise what innovative teaching and learning should look like at their school.

As principal, Nancy saw outstanding teaching and learning as key to engaging students in high-level thinking. Despite caring deeply about their students, the teachers needed support to incorporate ground-breaking teaching methods into their classrooms. They were also in need of a perspective shift; in her regular meetings with the teachers, Nancy worried that their expectations were not high enough. Results on provincial tests were much lower than report card scores, meaning that students who were getting acceptable marks at school were doing less well on tests geared to provincial standards. Over the course of about a year, the teachers compared their standards with exemplars published by the Ministry of Education. They compared how students were being marked on provincial tests to how they were being marked at the school. They worked with external consultants and board teaching-learning coaches to understand what was meant by rigorous achievement. Over time, the teachers came to realize that they were not expecting enough of their students, and began to see evidence that their students were capable of much, much more.

Many of the more useful tools to promote higher-order thinking have roots in Bloom et al.'s *Taxonomy of the Cognitive Domain*, first published in 1956.[13] This taxonomy organizes what teachers want students to know in a hierarchy from less to more complex. Simply remembering and understanding—as in memorizing the times tables or spelling—are at the bottom of the hierarchy. The ability of students to apply what they know is in the middle, and evaluating and creating are at the top. Too often, this taxonomy is seen as a step-by-step progression: first learn to remember, then apply, *then* create. Research shows, however, that when students engage in critical thinking and creating, they remember and understand better.[14] This is not only true in areas more traditionally recognized as creative, such as art or writing, but even in subjects like math and science. And it is true not just for supposedly advanced students, but for all of them.

Through this deeply honest investigation of their collective work, George Webster staff acknowledged that while they celebrated students' knowledge and understanding of basic skills, they rarely required students to apply these skills in new situations. Too often they let their students stop short of excellence because they worried that if they pushed them too hard, they would become frustrated and quit. In the name of kindness and caring, they were actually limiting their students, intervening too quickly and "rescuing" them from persevering through difficult challenges.

In this context, a group of interested teachers decided to work together on supporting all of their students in the development of higher-order math skills. Calling themselves the "Radical Math" group, the teachers used funding from the Model Schools program to bring in Professor Indigo Esmonde, an award-winning mathematics education scholar, and a few PhD students from the Ontario Institute for Studies in Education (OISE) to help with the initiative.

In its first year, the Radical Math group tested out the idea of teaching math through the exploration of real-world problems. Grade 5 teacher Ray McIntyre wondered how he could teach about capacity and volume using a social justice lens. His class, which included students whose families had recently arrived from Bangladesh, Sri Lanka and Pakistan, decided to examine how people in rural India managed their water supply. They studied wells (measuring the capacity of various buckets in the process), and simulated walking the average distance to a well carrying the weight of a water bucket. The challenge of this simulation spurred these low-income students on to action, and they set about raising money to fund a well in India. Ray built into this exploration activities that required students to measure capacity, volume, linear distance and mass, as well as work with decimals (in monetary sums) to reach their fundraising goal.

In year two, the Radical Math group was asked to join a monthly seminar on teaching through a culturally responsive lens at OISE's Centre for Urban Schooling, alongside educators from across the city. Model Schools funds were once again used to allow the teachers to benefit from this in-depth professional learning opportunity. Nancy participated in the seminar with her teachers. Alongside Ray McIntyre, they were joined by Dale Morris, a grade 1 teacher who had been at George Webster for a number of years; Rehanna Ayube and Steve Corke, two grade 2/3 teachers who worked across the hall from one another; and Robyn Coyle, who taught grade 4. With support from the seminar, the Radical Math group attempted to scale the previous year's classroom-level experiments up to a school-wide project that would allow students to deepen their knowledge of central math concepts while tackling a problem that affected their shared environment.

The first job was to identify a concern that students, staff and parents wanted to research together—something important, yet difficult, without easy answers. The Radical Math group reached out to students through a brainstorming session at the student council and through informal class discussions, to the school staff at their monthly meeting and to parents in hallway conversations at pickup. Almost everyone agreed: the biggest problem facing George Webster was student behaviour at recess and lunch.

By and large, students had good relationships with their teachers, and there was little trouble keeping order in the class-room, but a different picture emerged on the playground. In Nancy's first year at George Webster, a child and youth worker provided schoolyard programming to help build social skills. Unfortunately, due to cuts, the school lost funding for this worker, and what had been a trickle of discipline problems during recess and lunch became a steady flow. On occasion, these incidents would escalate into violence. Playground games would become heated as students suffered the indignities of losing, and without the direct supervision of an adult, some students lashed out with aggressive behaviour. In the classroom, teachers were trying to teach social skills, but some students had difficulty applying these lessons when adults were less available.

It did not help that Nancy was occasionally called out to the yard to break up fights between parents. There were varying examples of parental presence in the school—some parents pub-licly displayed poor conflict resolution skills and a suspicion of authority, others actively involved themselves in trying to build a safer environment for the kids. On one occasion, Nancy had to call the police when a father decided to discipline someone else's child by slapping her in the face.

A growing number of parents, however, had started to spend more time in the school, developing a sense of shared ownership and contributing to the improvement of children's lives there. Those parents volunteered in the nutrition programs and visited the parenting centre. Where once the school doors were locked, they were now open, with over a hundred parents and community members spending time each week reading with students, preparing snacks and lunches, and doing whatever they could to make the school a better place. The vast majority of the parents were excited by the new direction the school was taking, and were eager to support their children's learning. Some parents even asked Nancy if they could add themselves to the supervision roster at lunchtime and provide activities for the students to do that would keep them out of trouble.

Playground behaviour was adopted as the focus of the Radical Math project. Students from grades 1 to 5 became researchers. In a challenge connected directly to the data management strand of the math curriculum, which runs throughout the elementary years, the primary grades mapped out the playground, charting trees, tetherball courts, slides, baseball diamonds, monkey bars, and the field and pavement. Students then used sticky notes to annotate the map, depicting patterns of interaction. They identified parts of the playground where older students dominated and where English-language learners congregated; spots where girls played, as opposed to boys; spots where special education students spent most of their time. They discovered that grade 4s and 5s thought they owned the tarmac area where they played handball. Students identified the baseball diamond as an area where play sometimes got too rough and would erupt into fights. The school had a big field where students loved to play—there were small hills they enjoyed rolling down, and they felt safe falling down on the grass. But sometimes kids would play-fight at the bottom of those hills, and that fighting would turn into something more real.

Students surveyed each other about their experiences on the playground. Some classrooms devised questionnaires posing questions such as "What is your favourite game to play at recess?", "Have you ever experienced bullying at recess?" and "What equipment do you wish we had at recess?" Other classes wrote paragraphs completing the prompt: "When I think about recess I . . ." Answers varied from euphoric:

When I think about recess I think about my friend S. We always have fun together. At recess we play monkey bars. We also invite other friends to join us. Sometimes we play four squares. If there are puddles outside we jump over them. Me and S are best friends.

to troubling:

When I think about recess I think about the fite I hade at recess [sic].

to just plain funny:

When I think about recess I was playing with M. We were playing on the slide we were having fun me and M. We were doing crazy pug moves then we were trying to make each other laugh on the field then we took a walk we saw a boy that farts we started laughing then we were farting together.

The research was extensive, and involved a significant amount of data management. As questions arose, teachers, students and parents had to figure out ways to investigate them. While the students were in charge of the process, teachers provided essential support and direction for their learning. They helped students break down roadblocks, and taught key research methods concepts like sample size, reliability and validity.

Steve Corke, the grade 2/3 teacher, describes what he and his colleagues discovered from the students' research: "There was a kind of pecking order on the playground where the kids felt unsafe. We even discovered that girls felt uncomfortable in certain areas. It wasn't just a grade separation, the girls weren't allowed on the field by the boys." Although everyone had known that there was a problem *generally*, the students helped organize it into specific challenges requiring specific actions.

Once students had collected the data, their job was to work with the teachers to analyze it, and to find ways of representing their findings to other people. Written explanations were posted outside their classrooms so the whole community could see what they had found. Students were then encouraged to work creatively to devise plans to improve the situation—and to put their plans into action. Working with meaningful data they had generated themselves, the students moved naturally into higher-order skills like collective problem-solving, and were motivated and supported to communicate what they had learned and what they thought ought to be done.

It was in developing solutions to the complex problem that the students produced some really astounding results. Students in grades 1 to 3 wrote letters to Nancy, lobbying for more play equipment. Based on the students' recommendations, teachers took time to teach co-operative games in gym class, and the physical education teacher purchased kits of play equipment for each classroom. Rehanna Ayube, a grade 2/3 teacher, saw a direct correlation between the work on this project and students' desire to learn and their attitudes toward school:

> Writing a letter to the principal, and having the principal
> write them back, made that connection in the real world. It
> made things relevant to their lives, and you saw that interest
> sparked. . . . Having them express themselves about their
> lives engaged them, made them excited about school.

Students in older grades undertook even more ambitious projects based on their findings. Two students approached the librarian about opening the library during recess, to give students a quiet space to read. One group of grade 4 students analyzed anonymous data collected from the school's disciplinary records to better understand where and why playground problems were occurring. Every time a student was sent to the office, the teacher would fill out a discipline referral form, which stated why the student was sent, who was involved and what actions had already been taken to solve the problem. The principal or vice-principal would then use that form to record further actions, consequences and communication with families. The vice-principal had made a point of tallying particular characteristics like: Was the student involved a girl or a boy? Did the incident take place during class time, at morning recess, at lunch, at afternoon recess, before or after school? Did the incident take place in a classroom? In the hallway? In the bathroom? In the lunchroom? On the playground? Did the incident involve physical violence? Swearing? Threats? Stealing?

Anwar and Timothy, two boys in that grade 4 class, led the analysis of the office's disciplinary data. Anwar was born in the Middle East and had recently arrived at George Webster from another part of the city. A slight boy with a gentle smile and curly black hair, he was the protective and emotionally mature older brother of three siblings. He was not, however, an especially diligent student, and was happy to do the bare minimum. His partner, Timothy, was a blond, Canadian-born kid from a working-class family, also a responsible older brother who was not an especially strong student. And yet when the boys started investigating problems on the playground, something inside them was ignited.

Anwar and Timothy's initial conclusion was that more

incidents were happening at lunch and afternoon recess than in the morning. But they noticed that staff supervision of the playground was spread out equally throughout the day. They wondered if more staff could supervise in the afternoon. However, through a discussion with their teacher, they learned that there were no additional educators available for supervision. The teachers' collective agreement stated that teachers could not be assigned more than eighty minutes of supervision per week, and every teacher in the school had already been assigned the maximum. Anwar and Timothy found a solution to this roadblock. They reconfigured the duty schedule to place more teachers on the playground later in the day and fewer earlier. They also assigned the teachers strategic supervision positions that corresponded with those parts of the playground where problems seemed to occur most often—blind spots in the current duty schedule. They presented their solution to a group of representative teachers with a request to change the schedule and the placement of teachers in a way that still met the requirements of the collective agreement. The teachers unanimously agreed.

This was the first time in the known history of the school (perhaps the history of any school) when students had input on the supervision schedule. These two boys, who had never made much of an impression academically, had used their analytical powers to create a viable solution to an urgent problem, harnessing their presentation skills to persuade their teachers and making an exceptional contribution to the life of their school.

Another group of older students presented their thoughts on the playground problem to the student council. The student council was a recent addition to the school, constituted of about twenty-five students representing all grades and created to give students a voice in the governance of the school. The council met monthly with the administrative team to discuss issues of concern and to generate solutions (and eat cookies). The student council agreed with the group that approached them: students would get into fewer conflicts if they had more to do at lunch recess, which was four times as long as the other two recesses. The council thought more structured play would have a positive effect. The challenge was that teachers were already committed to extra-curricular activities, and most were not able to take on yet another big commitment. But there was another group of caring adults who would gladly help out if given direction: the growing core of parent volunteers. Nancy approached two of the parents who had asked how they could help, and they rounded up a group of interested parent volunteers. Together, they approached Right to Play, a global organization committed to promoting both child and community development through sport and games, and asked them to help train the students and their parents to lead co-operative games on the playground.

With support from Right to Play, teams of George Webster parents and students led games for about twenty minutes a day at lunch, several days a week. Sometimes, the students who had the most challenges behaviourally would take on the role of play leader. When given a job to do, these students were often able to be a part of the solution, instead of the problem. All this and other changes led to a reduction in discipline referrals to the office.

Through the ambitious, demanding playground math project, George Webster students developed their communication, team-work and leadership skills. Perhaps most significantly, the project fostered the belief that what the students had to say mattered, and that through their actions, they could make a positive difference in their community.

It is important to note that this project was just one aspect of the students' math program. Teachers used a mixture of direct instruction, problem-based learning and even drill to deliver the math curriculum in a balanced and varied way. But the inclusion of this big project required diverse, integrated skills, allowing teachers to engage their students in a new and meaningful way. And students responded. According to the Canadian Achievement Test, a norm-referenced, standardized test, the same students who had achieved below grade level in grade 2 math, and just at grade level in grade 3 at the beginning of that year, achieved well above their Canadian peers two years later.*

The enriched, integrated experiences offered at George Webster were happening at the same time that those who argue schools should be spending much more time on memorization of basic facts and on teacher-directed learning—the "basics" both in content and pedagogy—were becoming more vocal and politically active. Recently, after receiving a petition from seventeen thousand people, the Government of Alberta changed its curriculum to explicitly require students to memorize the times tables. Western Initiative for Strengthening Education in Mathematics (WISE Math), an advocacy group based in Winnipeg, has received media attention for demanding a much stronger emphasis on rote learning in math. Anna Stokke, the group's leader and the math professor we met at the opening of this chapter, wrote the following in *The Globe and Mail*:

_____

* Students who were at the school from grades 2 to 4 scored, on average, at the 1.4 level in grade 2 math (fall, 2010), and at the 6.2 level in grade 4 math (fall, 2012). Students who were at the school from grades 3 to 5 scored, on average, at the 3.2 level in grade 3 math (fall, 2010), and at the 5.7 level in grade 5 math (fall, 2012).

Too much math education is based on pet theories. . . .
Only direct instruction, routine practice and drill
significantly improved math achievement in struggling
math students. . . . Despite the evidence in favour of explicit
instruction and rigorous practice, discovery and inquiry-based
techniques dominate teacher education, professional
development and math textbooks. In other words, teachers
are frequently advised to use teaching techniques that do
not result in successful math learners.

Stokke cited a 2011 meta-analysis of 164 studies on the effectiveness of "discovery" (or student-led) learning, in which "explicit
instruction" was found to be a more effective instructional strategy than discovery learning that was unmediated by teachers.[15]
But Stokke neglected to mention the original study's main finding: that "guided discovery," in which students had a chance to
explore problems with support from a teacher, was found to be
the *most* effective teaching strategy of all.[16] In fact, after an
extensive review of the literature, the U.S. National Mathematics
Advisory Panel—widely viewed as a highly qualified if fairly conservative group—explicitly found that "high-quality research
doesn't support the contention that mathematics learning should
be entirely 'student centred' *or* 'teacher directed.'"[17]

Long-term, large-scale evaluations of the math curriculum in
the United States today compared to the more "traditional" one
implemented in the 1990s shed further light on student achievement. Like the curriculum in Canadian provinces, the newer U.S.
curriculum standards emphasize process over specific facts or
content. It focuses on mathematical reasoning, problem-solving
and communication through math, emphasizing connections
between math and the world. In Massachusetts, Minnesota and
Philadelphia, these evaluations—at the elementary, middle school

and secondary levels, using multiple, standardized assessments of achievement—showed students performing consistently on basic skills between the two curricula, but much better on higher-order tasks with the new curriculum. When teachers take a more conceptual, process-based approach, more students do well, fewer students do poorly and there is a reduction in racial differences in achievement.[18]

Arguing that math learning works best if the curriculum exposes students to big ideas and real-world connections does not mean that students should not be taught their times tables. Logic and neuroscience concur that a good command of basic operations—children in grades 2 and 3 being able to add and subtract in their heads "fluently, automatically," children in grade 5 being able to multiply without having to think about it—quite literally makes room in children's brains for them to focus on more advanced challenges. There *is* a place for teacher-directed learning in schools, as we saw at George Webster. There is strong evidence to show that, particularly when students are struggling with math, they benefit from explicit instruction, including clear models, opportunities for practice, the chance to "think aloud" and regular feedback.[19] At George Webster, while the teachers were involved in the playground project, they continued to teach using textbooks, workbooks and games to reinforce basic skills. Students who needed extra support, practice or guided instruction were tutored after school, invited to extra-help sessions during recess and given the opportunity to work with a small group or individually with the teacher as needed.

These insights about math mirror those in literacy. In reading, direct instruction in phonics is a critical strategy for the significant number of children for whom reading does not come easily. Yet those same, struggling students *also* need exposure to real books and engaging stories that make reading exciting and help build the vocabulary and understanding that are essential parts of literacy.

The idea that mastery of basic skills should precede the opportunity to think about bigger math concepts—or even, in the most extreme cases, replace it—can be a barrier to students engaging more meaningfully with math. The work of George Webster's teachers followed the best practices, as identified by the U.S. National Academies of Science, for developing a robust group of science, technology, engineering and math (STEM) learners prepared to lead the next technological and knowledge breakthrough. The National Academies conclude that "effective instruction capitalizes on students' early interest and experiences, identifies and builds on what they know, and provides them with experiences to engage them in the practices of science and sustain their interest."[20]

As Steve Corke explained, "The students realized they could be part of the process of their learning. They were driving the learning. . . . Kids who normally might not be that engaged became engaged." Robin Coyle, the grade 4 teacher, remarked, "It's probably the most exciting thing I've done in my teaching career."

High Expectations Are the Key to Possibilities for All Children
What is perhaps most dangerous about the idea that students should hold off on too much exploration, application or problem-solving until the basics are mastered, is that a basics-only diet is most often prescribed to students who come from disadvantaged backgrounds. Too often, due to teachers' low expectations of them, students who are missing out on many of society's opportunities are also deprived of the learning experiences that tap into higher-order skills.[21] Unfortunately, there is a very strong body of research that shows low expectations are distinctly harmful to children's learning and development.

This research dates back to 1968, when in a famous and ethically controversial experiment, a group of researchers gave teachers false information about the IQs of students in their class. The students whom teachers *expected* to perform well, due to the false perception that their IQs were higher, ultimately showed significantly larger gains in intellectual growth at the end of one year.[22] In another study, research revealed that a group of New Zealand teachers expected less from their Maori students than their existing levels of achievement suggested, and more from their East Asian, Pacific Islander and Caucasian students. By the end of year, the Maori students' achievement had fallen behind.[23] Other research meta-analyses, crunching the results of dozens of studies, shows that high expectations are the form of parent involvement with the biggest impact on students' academic achievement.[24]

In addition, high or low expectations also translate, very directly, into structures at school—students may be exposed to different material, and streamed into different programs, depending on judgments about their abilities. Teachers may construe the same behaviour differently: in a child they perceive as capable, teachers may interpret a silence as reflection, whereas in one they see as less capable, it may be read as ignorance. These low expectations can have direct bearing on where students will wind up after graduation. High expectations, and ensuring students have access to work that reflects them, have been found to be a prerequisite for high achievement.[25]

As the George Webster staff demonstrated, high expectations for all students, despite past performance or privilege, and a demand that they engage with higher-level thinking, can be a foundation for success. Relegating basics-based learning to marginalized students because of a lack of confidence in their ability only serves to reinforce structures of inequality.

Mi'kmaw Kina'matnewey and the "Show Me Your Math" Project

Nova Scotia's residential school, Shubenacadie Indian Residential School—where in the 1940s and '50s, the Canadian government conducted experiments on malnourished Indigenous children,[26] among other human rights violations—closed in 1967. But the province's education system remained mired in racism for many years. The system may or may not have met the needs of the general population, but it consistently failed to meet the demands of Indigenous students and their communities. John Jerome Paul would go on to become the director of programs for Mi'kmaw Kina'matnewey (MK), the Indigenous educational authority in Nova Scotia. He recalls being punished for speaking Mi'kmaq by the priest who ran the local Indian day school, and being turned off by a curriculum designed to train him to become a farm worker—the only work most educators thought him capable of. His experiences were common among Indigenous children of his generation.

In 1989, a Royal Commission into the wrongful murder conviction of Donald Marshall Jr. found that both the justice and education systems were tainted by racism against the Mi'kmaq. In the wake of that report and community activism, the right of Mi'kmaw communities in Nova Scotia to govern their own education system was formally recognized by federal legislation in 1998. The new law empowered and funded local communities to run K–12 education and created MK, led by the chiefs to act as a unique education authority across the thirteen communities. One of the first things the chiefs did was ask themselves what it would mean to create an education system that respected their language and culture. Even the organization's name reflects a deep shift in philosophy, describing "the process of educating our people from birth to grave."

Lisa Lunney Borden, a math teacher and scholar who started

teaching in Mi'kmaw schools in 1995 and is the chair of the Department of Teacher Education at St. Francis Xavier University, states that MK's central goal is "to cover the curriculum and be as good as the public schools, but to change the approach." Sometimes, that means intensive personal supports and mentorship. Above all, staff are challenged to bring the community into every classroom, using the knowledge of their elders to inform instruction, and ensuring that learning is relevant and congruent to Mi'kmaw culture and language. This challenge led Lunney Borden to transform the way she teaches—and thinks about—math.

A white Canadian, Lunney Borden often asked her students: "What's the word for . . ." and "Is there a word for. . . ." She quickly began to understand that there are concepts in Mi'kmaq that do not exist in English, and vice versa. One example she uses to illustrate this idea is the word *flat*. When she asked elders how to say *flat* in Mi'kmaq, they asked her how she was using the word. Depending on its meaning, there are different Mi'kmaq translations. There is one word for "it can sit still." There is another word for "you can put things on it." Over time, Lunney Borden realized that the Mi'kmaw language conceives of math in a way that emphasizes doing and motion, as opposed to English, which tends to be more static. She began to "verbify" math and to pay more attention to motion and spatial reasoning. Spatial reasoning is concerned with the location and movement of objects and ourselves, either mentally or physically in space.[27] Imagining objects moving in space, composing and decomposing shapes, and understanding the relationship between three-dimensional and two-dimensional shapes are all examples of spatial thinking. In teaching these concepts to her students, Lunney Borden was able to reach them in a new way. She explains, "We are learning that spatial reasoning interventions are more effective than numeracy interventions. Students who are getting extra support in spatial reasoning are progressing in leaps and bounds—their math abilities are increasing exponentially."

John Jerome Paul is convinced that many students have to learn that "math is not a European concept." He says the priority in each community plan is to develop its own people, by asking, "What would keep a student interested in learning about something? How will they see, hey, this is about me, I can relate to this stuff?"

Lunney Borden worked with her students on a project called "Show Me Your Math," which engaged students in culturally based inquiry projects like discovering how to bead Wampum belts; plant medicine gardens; and make maple syrup, snowshoes and canoe paddles. Some students learned to create canoe paddles from their grandfathers. These men were canoe racers, but they had come to racing only as adults. Colonization and the cycle of poverty had prohibited the grandfathers from learning these skills as children. Later in life, however, they reclaimed this traditional practice and learned both to race and to carve paddles. As Lunney Borden tells it, "The men found being involved in the students' education empowering, as if they were 'getting something back.'" Creating the paddles gave students opportunities to practise measurement and geometry in a real-life situation that had both meaning and consequence.

A Show Me Your Math report describes a unit taught by an elder, Dianne, who makes circular quill boxes using cultural knowledge, facilitating a conversation about the concept of pi:

> She explained that she made quill boxes by beginning with a circle top and starting her pattern in the centre. She then explained that she made the ring for the top from strips of wood. To ensure the ring was the right size, Dianne said she would measure three times across the circular top and add a

thumb. She claimed this would make a perfect ring every time.[28]

This particular unit gave students an opportunity to explore the role of measurement, geometry and patterns in the creation of quill work, a cultural practice that is at risk of being lost. Students learned about math at the same time that they learned about their own culture, and how to preserve it.

Aaron Prosper, whom we met in the introduction, remembers a Show Me Your Math project he took on in grade 7, based on the Mi'kmaw game of Waltes. The game requires a carved thirty-centimetre bowl, five dice-like objects traditionally carved of walrus tusk or caribou antler, and fifty-one counting sticks. Aaron's project involved not only calculating the probability of different throws of the dice, but also looking at how the geometry of the bowl affected how the dice would fall.

For Aaron, it was particularly meaningful because the bowls, filled with water, had traditionally been used as a way of reading visions, and to settle disputes or make decisions. During colonization, priests would drill holes into the bowls—purportedly to make them more "aerodynamic" during a game of Waltes—while in actuality inhibiting their spiritual purpose. "The priests' claim was kind of ridiculous, if you understand physics," explains Aaron. The project not only had him doing quite complex math—it gave him a new tool to understand and critique a historical example of racism.

Tiannie Paul, another student from our introduction, remembers being expected to share not only math calculations in class, but what she had learned from her community about the concept at hand. In grade 4, Tiannie interviewed elders about the eight-pointed star that is a symbol of Mi'kmaw culture as part of her geometry program. In grade 5, she gave a Show Me Your Math presentation on Kraft Dinner and hot dogs, a project that involved measuring proportions and boiling points—and making everybody laugh. The project won the MK-wide grade 5 math prize. Students were encouraged to explore their traditional culture and to bring their own interests and daily life into school.

Together, MK and St. Francis Xavier University have certified 160 educators to teach culturally based math. MK ensures that every one of their schools has a math leader, supported by a math consultant, and Lunney Borden is actively involved in providing support to these educators. The perfect storm of teaching math in a system that is committed to overcoming a damaging legacy of colonialism, by a committed group of mostly Indigenous educators working with strong support from the local university, has helped create a model for First Nations communities across Canada—and for schools everywhere.

According to John Jerome Paul, high expectations have been a crucial part of MK's success. "One thing we always stressed to people—there is no 'hoping' you will survive in our program. We *expect* you to do well. We've helped you develop those core skills that you need—now it's really you that needs to take the next steps."

Through high expectations and higher-order thinking extended to students at a systems level, MK has made great strides in closing achievement gaps. There are thirteen Mi'kmaw nations in Nova Scotia, with a population of over sixteen thousand.[29] In 2016, 87 percent of Mi'kmaw students in those communities graduated from high school.[30] That result is more than double the auditor general's 2011 assessment of the graduation rate of First Nations students on reserves across Canada (41 percent), and within 1 percent of the graduation rate of all students in Nova Scotia.[31]

Looking for the schools of the future must start with looking at the schools and systems that are overcoming some of the greatest challenges now. This highly successful school system shows that there is no trade-off between learning math basics and learning the skills needed to face the future with feet firmly rooted in one's own culture. In fact, these approaches are mutually reinforcing.

To navigate their futures, students will need to conquer math. The key to doing so is an education that provides them with the basics while simultaneously pushing them to apply these skills to the real world. For teachers, working from students' knowledge and strengths creates a pathway to unfamiliar and more demanding material. Schools, too, must build upon what they know in order to handle the unknowns of a fast-changing future—a challenge that requires a strong foundation, confidence and, as we will see in the next chapter, considerable creativity.

TWO

TEACHING CREATIVITY

"Creativity and education sit and look at one another from a distance much like the boys and girls at the seventh-grade dance, each one knowing that a foray across the gym floor might bring great rewards but is fraught with peril."
—JEFFERY K. SMITH AND LISA F. SMITH,
"Educational Creativity" in
The Cambridge Handbook of Creativity[1]

At Douglas Park Elementary School in Regina, Saskatchewan, twelve-year-old Chloe wanted to learn about her ancestors. She went online to find a genealogy website, but ran into various difficulties—some cost money, and others didn't have the answers she sought. Undeterred, she tried a different strategy. She went to her grandparents' house to interview them about their family history, plotting their memories into a family tree of her own crafting.

In the very same grade 7 class, Isaac—a boy who has always loved video games—decided to build one of his own with a friend. He already knew a bit of coding, but creating a video game would require him to master a new, more complex program. Even as he progressed, there were setbacks. On the school's well-used computers, his files kept getting corrupted, so that he had to start again repeatedly. "Just another speedbump on the road," he explained. "You have to figure out how to work around it, try to fix it, do something so you can keep going." By the end of the term, he had developed a chase game where his characters jumped and leaped across a background of houses, trees and a terrain that shifted as they moved.

Chloe and Isaac were self-taught, working on projects they themselves dreamed up. Behind their creative exploration was a

teacher, Aaron Warner. Warner has built creativity into his classroom. "Genius Hour" is dedicated time for his students to pursue
anything about which they are passionate, learning in their own
way. It is loosely based on the model developed at Google, where
software engineers were expected to spend up to 20 percent of
their paid time working on their own ideas. "Twenty-percent
time" projects led to the development of Gmail and Adsense, the
advertising software that contributes approximately a quarter of
the company's vast revenue. Warner's Genius Hour builds the
same principle into the classroom, with students devoting two
hours a week to their creative endeavours.

Warner learned about Genius Hour through his online professional learning community, comprised of educators from
across the country and as far away as Australia. Every summer,
Warner and his group read a book and discuss it on Twitter. Their
first book was A.J. Juliani's *Innovation and Inquiry in the
Classroom*, which addresses what the media sometimes call a
"creativity crisis." It provides practical guidance to teachers trying to implement Genius Hour projects in their classrooms, from
harnessing the support of other teachers, parents and students
who think "this is awesome," to reassuring those whose position
is "this is great, but . . .", to reaching out to those who think "this
is crazy." The book has advice for teachers on how to prepare
their class, how to support students, and how to approach and
evaluate their final products.

As they engaged with the book, the teachers in the online
community wrestled with various questions. If they encouraged
students to do self-directed work, how would they assess it?
Should students get a mark for following their passions? If they
did not, how would they as teachers communicate students'
learning to their school leadership and to parents? The group discussed highlighting some of the skills built into, and exercised

through, creative endeavours, like non-fiction writing and research skills, to demonstrate what their students were learning. As their summer of discussion came to a close, a group of teachers, including Warner, committed to adopting Genius Hour.

When he brought Genius Hour into the classroom, Warner had imagined that "magic would take place," but when he invited students to do whatever they wanted, telling them "the sky's the limit," their first question was: "What do you want me to do?" Often, contemporary teaching emphasizes clear, measureable outcomes, detailed rubrics and step-by-step directions. The goal may be transparency, to break tasks down and to help students learn to self-assess, but often it can feel like students are being schooled in following instructions. In this context, it is a bit unsettling to be told: "You can do anything you want to."

It was a pretty big hurdle. Warner went back to his Twitter community to ask for examples of what was happening in their classrooms. A high school science teacher shared a list of Genius Hour projects from his class that included understanding the circulatory system of a horse, how babies form inside the belly, how to build a small engine, how brain cancer spreads, how to improve hand–eye coordination, and what causes us to forget, as well as contemplating whether Big Foot exists (which included studying the history of the myth). That teacher confessed that not all of the ideas were particularly good ones, but he thought that having students learn that fact for themselves—experience failure and move on—was an important part of the hour.

The kids in Warner's class came up with their own ideas—although at first they were not particularly ambitious. One student wanted to learn to serve a volleyball. Another wanted to learn how to make Rice Krispies squares. But with practice and encouragement over the course of the year, the kids started to think bigger. Some of the students were most enthusiastic about what they could *teach* each other, and how to make learning exciting. One student borrowed the school board's projection tent to use as a mini-planetarium in order to teach her classmates about black holes.

The more they discovered their own potential, the more excited the students grew. And in year two, with a new group of students who had heard about the previous year's class and had had a chance to wrap their heads around the idea, the start-up period was much shorter. It wasn't just the kids who were paying attention. The other grade 7/8 teacher incorporated Genius Hour into her classroom, and then the grade 6/7 teachers tasked their students with developing self-directed "action plans" as a part of their health curriculum. Warner started working with teachers across the school division through a twice-yearly professional development "EdCamp," where he supported (and continues to support) them in bringing Genius Hour into their schools.

After pitching their ideas at the start of the school year, Warner's students use goal-setting sheets and agendas to set specific plans of action for every Genius Hour session. Warner does his best to review these plans with the students before each session begins. During the hour, he circulates within the school, "helping where [he] can," but trying to stay pretty hands off. Few students stay in the classroom during the two hours a week dedicated to Genius Hour. At one point, Warner had a couple of students working downstairs in the school kitchen, another outside practising his fastball against a pitching net, and Isaac and his partner off in the library working together on their video game. At least some of the time, students are working on things that Warner does not know how to do—so he offers moral support and helps come up with workarounds when students hit glitches.

The students also help each other, even when their projects don't seem to have much in common. When Isaac was stuck and frustrated with his computer game, he got help from Abby, who was learning to crochet using YouTube and her church's knitters' club as resources. "I don't know what you would call it," Abby explained. "Being able to figure things out yourself, make a plan, know what you are going to do . . . maybe leadership? We don't just take notes, we get to make things and be more creative—to try new things."

Another key part of Warner's strategy is to share his students' work, posting projects on the classroom website and on Twitter, holding a mirror to students' success and sharing it with the world.

There is a sense of urgency around Warner's innovative classroom projects. Genius Hour exercises skills often underused and undervalued in our education system: it allows students to stretch their imaginations, follow their own whims and curiosities, and define their own measures of achievement. It helps kids find different ways to succeed at an age when many are struggling with what success means. Genius Hour provides them with an opportunity to achieve outside the traditional borders of academia, and can actually bolster their confidence and engagement in the classroom.

The other reason Warner is committed to making space for creativity in the classroom is related to the larger world. Creativity is a vital life skill. It doesn't just enrich day-to-day life; it is key to job-readiness in the broadest sense. As Warner notes, "Sixty percent of the jobs of the future haven't been invented yet." This insight echoes Sir Ken Robinson's argument, in the most-watched TED Talk of all time, titled "Do Schools Kill Creativity?". Robinson made the case that creativity is central to developing education that will "take us into a future we can't grasp." Robinson believes that we must take seriously the fact that we cannot know what the world will look like. He is an advocate for school systems where creativity is considered as important as literacy and afforded the same status. There is a yawning need for original thinking to solve current and future problems—and original work will not happen unless children are prepared both to take risks and to put the tremendous talents with which they are born to use, rather than, as Robinson put it, "squandering them ruthlessly" through a standards-based education and narrow academic focus.[2]

Can Creativity Be Taught and Measured?

The standard definition of creativity is the generation of novel ideas or products. Creativity has also been defined as openness to exploration and as divergent thinking, which is the ability to generate numerous, diverse options or solutions. Creativity exists across traditional academic disciplines. While you can easily identify it in the fine arts, creativity is also a key aspect of domains as wide-ranging as business strategy, mathematical theory and cooking.

Creativity is recognized as a critical "twenty-first century skill" by business groups, arts groups and international organizations like UNESCO and the Organisation for Economic Co-operation and Development (OECD). It is seen as essential to a rich and satisfying life, to the generation of new art and useful technologies, and to the solution of the world's problems. Exercising creativity can also help to better prepare us emotionally for the unpredictable—training us to innovate and problem-solve on the fly, and strengthening our ability to take calculated risks.

Before becoming an international intellectual celebrity, Sir Ken Robinson chaired a national committee tasked with reviewing creativity and culture in British education. The resulting report, *All Our Futures*,[3] wrestled with the challenges of trying to institutionalize creativity in the school system. Part of the challenge, the committee acknowledged, was achieving widespread recognition of creativity's importance—another was determining how to actively change practices in schools. In an education environment dominated by test scores, boosting the status of creativity as one of schools' core activities means working hard to challenge the primacy of measurable outcomes in the education system. This process is not simple—it requires, for example, an approach to assessment that *encourages* students to make mistakes. You can't "teach" creativity standing in front of a classroom, and "judging" a creative process or output is more complicated than marking a test. And there are differences in how people *perceive* creativity. To be creative, does something have to be completely original? In order to teach creativity, must schools mandate that their students produce a breakthrough in existing knowledge, or is a more permissive definition of creativity possible?

James Kaufman and Ronald Beghetto, cognitive psychologists who work at the University of Connecticut, are best known for developing a scale for creative acts, and in 2010 they co-edited *Nurturing Creativity in the Classroom*.[4] Kaufman has been a leader in the study of creativity as a core aspect of psychology, and Beghetto has specialized in studying creativity in the classroom. Their scale begins with what they call "mini-c creativity": essentially, the pursuit of a creative project for personal enrichment. One step up is "little-c creativity," which involves some mastery of a creative process. "Pro-c creativity" refers to creativity conducted on a professional level: graphic design; architecture; professional dancing, writing, or making a living as a musician. "Big-c creativity" is the stuff of legends: the discovery of the double helix, or the musical legacies of Mozart and the Beatles. Right now, schools mostly work in the range of mini-c and little-c creativity, although they can be given the tools to lay the groundwork for pro-c and even perhaps big-c creativity.

A comprehensive school in central London, U.K., has been actively nurturing its students' creativity across the curriculum for the past fifteen years.

Thomas Tallis School has about 1,900 students, drawn from both a rundown council housing estate and one of the wealthiest neighbourhoods in South East London. The school has participated in a pilot project coming out of the Centre for Real-World Learning at Winchester University, which tests the disruptive idea that the development of creativity can be *measured* in students.

Jon Nichols, Thomas Tallis's director of creativity and arts (a newly created leadership position that signals the school's commitment to fostering innovation), was at first fairly skeptical about whether creativity could, or should, be measured. He doesn't think progress in creativity is particularly linear— some days you are more creative than others. And besides, he notes, "creativity is not a very healthy thing to want to measure anyway." He argues that measuring creativity is part of the troubling trend in education policy of "wanting to quantify everything all the time." But when he met the Real-World Learning researchers, he was intrigued by their ideas, and compelled by the opportunity to offer his colleagues greater expertise in how to teach creativity.

The Real-World Learning group had spent several years developing a tool that could be used by teachers to assess creative work and provide direction for further creative development. Creativity is not a specific learning expectation in the U.K., so they knew their tool would need to be really useful, relevant and accessible to teachers—because it would otherwise be easy to ignore. Ultimately, the researchers decided to focus on identifying key "habits" of creativity—diverse traits intrinsic to the act of creation that teachers could work to cultivate and evaluate.

They identified five main habits, each defined by three traits, for educators to promote and assess. Being *inquisitive* is one of these habits, and is defined by wondering and questioning, exploring and investigating, and challenging assumptions. Being *imaginative* is another, associated with playing with possibilities, making connections and using intuition. *Persistence* involves sticking with difficult tasks, daring to be different and tolerating uncertainty. *Discipline* is defined by developing technique, reflecting critically, crafting and improving. And finally, because creativity is fundamentally social, *collaboration* is an important habit: sharing products and sharing feedback, and co-operating appropriately. Teachers could track their students' development using the metrics depicted in Figure 1[5], measuring whether their habits were awakening (very little development), accelerating (a bit), advancing (a fair bit) or adept (a lot).

During the course of the pilot project, the list of habits gave teachers a focus and allowed them to concentrate on teaching traits they had not typically promoted explicitly before. They struggled, however, with assessment. They were much more comfortable looking at effort than at progress, even when using friendly, non-judgmental measures like awakening, accelerating, advancing and adept. The school decided, consequently, to leave the strict measuring system behind. Instead, the students were asked to assess their own efforts, which were then measured against their teachers' impressions, with regular check-ins scheduled to address any discrepancies. Conversations that start with, "Oh, I didn't notice that—can you give me an example of when you challenged an assumption?" have proved very constructive. Parents, too, have appreciated receiving parallel reports on their children's achievement: not simply measureable test results but

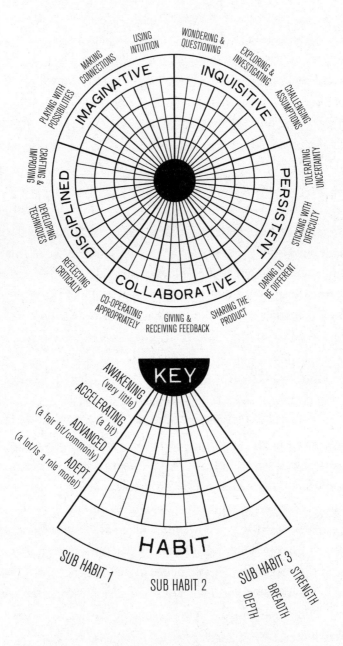

FIGURE 1. Centre for Real-World Learning: Prototype for
Assessing Creative Dispositions, Field Trial Tool

also reports on the efforts taken to build positive habits around learning and creating. And moving from a rigid assessment system to a more collaborative—and creative—measure of creativity has allowed students to experiment and explore with greater risk and ingenuity.

The halls of Thomas Tallis are adorned with murals identifying the habits so central to the school's vision, habits that have become a focus of every course, across all the curriculum areas, with entire seven-week terms devoted to mastering one particular habit at a time. In a history class, in a recent term emphasizing collaboration, the class used digital tools to develop a shared set of notes that everyone could access—a form of classroom-based crowd-sourcing.

The embrace of the habits sometimes leads to innovative collaborations across disciplines. The year 11 science students were assigned the task of teaching year 9s how to dissect a rat. In turn, the year 9s were charged with documenting and reflecting on the process with video, painting and drawing in their art class, ultimately creating a shared exhibition for the school's open house.

The Real-World Learning Centre's research project is still in relatively early stages, but by taking creativity seriously enough to try to measure it, the researchers have launched important dialogues. The centre has been singled out by the OECD for helping schools take an intentional approach toward developing this so-called twenty-first-century skill.

Teaching Creativity at John Polanyi Collegiate Institute

The principal of Toronto's John Polanyi Collegiate Institute, Aiman Flahat, was one of Canada's Outstanding Principals in 2012, and a leader at the forefront of creative education.

Flahat was born in Jordan and moved to Canada at age eleven. Like many newcomers, Flahat's parents looked for work during the day and studied English at night. Both health care profession-als, his parents made huge sacrifices for their children, and Flahat was determined to do his part. He struggled with English, how-ever, and when the time came to enter high school, his guidance teacher insisted he could not succeed in academic courses, and advised him to select classes that could provide him with a voca-tional future instead. The practice of directing students into courses with different content and pedagogy based on their perceived abilities or future goals is called "streaming." Flahat remembers his guidance teacher saying, "You will not be suc-cessful. You will not achieve." His parents pushed back, and Flahat felt driven to achieve, partly to prove the teacher wrong. The family insisted that their son be allowed to take academic courses, and he did—with considerable success, his language skills soon catching up.

Flahat has a keen awareness of the power of a good high school education, where streaming is only one of the processes that can be a real factor in determining students' future achieve-ment. While almost all students enter high school thinking they will go on to post-secondary education, by the time they leave, aspirations are often quite different. Flahat understands that high expectations of students are critical, particularly in inner-city settings. A key means of implicitly communicating high expectations is by exposing students to the kinds of advanced skills that have been identified as being essential for future success—creativity among them.

John Polanyi Collegiate Institute, just northwest of downtown Toronto, first opened its doors in September 2011. Residents in Lawrence Heights, the surrounding neighbourhood, are predomi-nantly first-generation immigrants from East and West African countries, the Caribbean and Latin America. There are 1,080 public housing family units there, and a high proportion of single-parent families, with an average annual household income of fifteen thousand dollars. The community is also deeply affected by youth gangs and violent crime involving firearms (although specific statistics are difficult to come by because the neighbourhood is part of a much larger police division, dubbed "Toronto's murder capital" by *The Globe and Mail* in 2009[6]). Another local principal expressed frustration about the neighbourhood's bad reputation overshadowing the strengths of the community. But he acknowledged, "There are one or two major shootings in this area every year, and the impact on the students is enormous." For Flahat, these circumstances are all the more reason to teach students "how to think and be able to solve big problems while maintaining a vision, being optimistic and not settling for the easy fixes."

When Flahat became principal in January 2012, John Polanyi was under-subscribed, with only about three hundred students. The school was located on the site of the former Bathurst Heights School, which had closed ten years earlier due to low enrolment. In an effort to attract more students, the TDSB had reopened the site but rebranded it as a collegiate and named it after John Polanyi, a Canadian scientist who won the Nobel Prize in Chemistry for his research in chemical kinetics. John Polanyi Collegiate Institute was determined to attract students with aspirations of post-secondary studies—the best and the brightest from Lawrence Heights, the adjacent communities and beyond—and to become a centre of excellence in the sciences, mathematics and robotics.

In one particularly striking commitment to raising expectations for its students, Flahat and his team forged a partnership with one of the world's most highly regarded business schools, the Rotman School of Management at the University of Toronto. Former dean Roger Martin had developed a creative problem-solving methodology he calls "integrative thinking." Martin had interviewed over fifty business leaders while conducting research for his best-selling business book, *The Opposable Mind: Winning Through Integrative Thinking*. He profiled leaders like Michael Lee-Chin, the billionaire investor and philanthropist who grew up the child of store clerks in Jamaica, and Martin's long-time client CEO Alan Lafley of Procter and Gamble. Martin's book decodes the process these leaders use to think through problems. The best thinkers, he argues, can hold two opposing ideas (or solutions) in their head at the same time, then synthesize to get the best of both. When Lafley started at Procter and Gamble, for example, he faced two competing strains of advice on how to manage the challenge of declining revenues. Some advocated cost-cutting and price wars with competing brands; others advocated investment in research and development. Lafley chose an approach that incorporated both methods, focusing on reorganization with an emphasis on reducing cost, and acquisition of smaller companies that were pioneering innovative products.

As the dean of a business school, Martin was convinced that higher education often trains students in analytical methodologies that actually work *against* the kind of creative synthesis he had seen to be a hallmark of successful business people. He sought to develop this skill in his students, teaching the approach to MBAs and commerce students. But he began to think, "Why are we waiting so long? Doing integrative thinking in business school is remedial. Let's start teaching this *before* we have to 'undo the damage' of more conventional education." His team decided to "take the business out of it" and see if their program, called I-Think, had legs in the K–12 sector.

His team partnered with a handful of elite private schools, offering the program as an after-school extracurricular. The program spread to other private schools. As it gained buzz, the TDSB approached Rotman about bringing the program into public schools, especially those where students were facing significant challenges. One of those schools was John Polanyi. Flahat welcomed the chance to offer I-Think to his students: "Our goal was that where you are will not determine where you're going. . . . We wanted to ensure that opportunities were created at John Polanyi, because students from the community have all the talents and abilities, but sometimes are just lacking opportunity."

John Polanyi incorporated the I-Think program into a grade 12 business credit called Creative Problem Solving, and made sure the opportunity was available to all students. Rahim Essabhai, an experienced teacher in the school's business department, worked with a research associate (and certified teacher) from Rotman, Nogah Kornberg, to bring the course to life. Instead of using a textbook, they built a binder of articles from psychology and business journals, annotated with detailed lesson plans. They developed assignments that encouraged students to show the stages of their thinking and that also "made learning real."

Essabhai is the "CEO" of his classroom, and his students work as consultants for the real-world clients with whom he pairs them. For example, he has connected his class with Rouge National Urban Park, in Scarborough, which wanted a team of students to advise them on their challenge of ensuring that urban youth use the park. He also paired them with Wounded Warriors, an organization that provides support to ill and injured veterans, which was interested in broadening its range of participants, and particularly in boosting the participation of women veterans. A team of his students also worked with a group of personal care assistants in a nursing home to develop an approach to address their stress levels. Some of his students have gone out to find their own "clients," such as rabbit rescue organization Rescue Angels Society, which wanted advice on becoming better established and a more effective advocate for animal rights. Some years, Flahat gives the students a specific challenge that could serve to improve their school. He asked one class to try to use their creative problem-solving skills to build enrolment. They had already gone from three hundred students to seven hundred. What would it take to get to a thousand?

Sakaana Yasotharan, whom we met in the introduction, was one of the grade 12 students charged with increasing enrolment. Over the course of five weeks, Sakaana and her classmates used the integrative thinking methodology to wrestle with their problem. They identified two opposing models for boosting enrolment: offering niche appeal through specialized programs and becoming a community hub. Students needed to recognize—and live with—the competing strengths of the two models.

The students were asked to identify potential stakeholders, gather information from them and develop "pro-pro" lists in which they identified the benefits of their two models for these individuals. This step in the methodology was designed to force the students to consider multiple perspectives before developing a model that, ideally, would synthesize their two opposing approaches. Sakaana's group spoke to a vice-principal at Jarvis Collegiate, a school that had attracted students on the basis of a strong academic record. They also spoke to a community organizer in Regent Park, a low-income area going through a major mixed-income redevelopment. Sakaana remembers visiting the reconfigured community and thinking the redevelopment was a great idea. But when she talked to the organizer, she learned how difficult it was to convince people to come out to events in the new facilities. With the transformation in the area, "it didn't feel like home for them." This insight made Sakaana want to develop structures within her own school that would both attract new students and ensure a sense of comfort and community for all.

Kornberg remembers Sakaana's group struggling. They were more immediately drawn toward the community model because they saw how it responded to the needs of their neighbourhood. They worried the specialized school model was really about enticing students who *weren't* like them. Sakaana remembers her group wondering, "What do kids from well-off families have that low-income students don't?" and "Why should we want those kids here?" They came to some uncomfortable answers. In sports, for example, wealthier kids could be coming from rep teams that had had more coaching and opportunity to practice, making them stronger athletes. They may also have parents who could sponsor school teams. "We have kids who are great athletes, but they can't afford to play rep," she paused, "In the beginning, this [realization] was a total hit to our self-esteem."

Sakaana had herself chosen to attend John Polanyi because of the academic advantages she thought it would give her. And she had excelled there. The school's vision, after all, was about unlocking the unlimited potential of its students. Despite this, Sakaana and her classmates seem to have internalized some low expectations, and to have assumed that the kinds of students who would boost their school would be different from themselves. The teachers challenged the group to ask themselves what positive factors might push their principal to consider specializing their school, *assuming* he had the current students' best interests at heart. The topic of the project consumed Sakaana, and she began thinking about it all the time, "even at breakfast." Her "a-ha moment," came in relation to her own biases: "I started to think about why I had them. Was it because of my exposure to the media? I began to question my own thinking. I began thinking about thinking."

The students had to condense all of their contemplation and discussion into two words that described the central strengths of each potential solution. Sakaana's group chose *mastery* for the specialized school model, and the Swahili word *ubuntu* for the community hub model. They considered mastery to be a vital skill, and identified excelling at something as a valuable way to gain confidence; despite their initial suspicion of the specialized schools model, the students were eventually able to identify its assets, and what it could offer them. *Ubuntu* has been translated as, "I am who I am because we are who we are." John Polanyi, they concluded, would increase its enrolment by supporting the development of both confidence and excellence (mastery) and a thriving, inclusive community (*ubuntu*).

At the end of the term, the I-Think students presented their work in the sleek, ultra-modern Rotman business school—a significant social distance from Lawrence Heights, if only a few stops away by subway. The group was allowed ten PowerPoint slides to present their idea, and was required to use nine of them to illustrate the process by which they had arrived at their recommendation. Sakaana and her group proposed melding mastery and *ubuntu* by emphasizing each at different points in the curriculum. In their view, the school's youngest and oldest students, those in grades 9 and 12, should take a non-streamed course together, through which they would work to make things better in the school—to build aspects of *ubuntu*, especially in the key transition years of high school. The course would be a chance to explore individual identity and to enrich the community. Further, students in grades 10 and 11 should receive a focus on mastery, through exposure to co-op programs and other specialized offerings.

One of the judges at the Rotman presentation was Roger Martin. He told the students that their presentation was one of the best he had seen, at any level of education. Martin commented on the success of the program more generally, too: "These are kids who are handed tough, intractable problems in this world. When you see what they can do with a workmanlike approach to solving them, a reasonable methodology, stamina for the roadblocks and frustrations—combined with real insights. . . . It makes you feel confident for humanity."

Flahat was also inspired by his students' ideas, and took their solutions seriously. Working with his staff, he pulled various strands from the students' proposal and wove them into the life of the school. Sakaana's group's desire to incorporate the values of *ubuntu* aligned with his own vision for John Polanyi: "Creating a culture that is welcoming, and makes students feel empowered, rather than just getting things done, managing."

Galvanized by the students' proposal, Flahat and his staff created two new courses to allow students to exercise both *ubuntu* and mastery. They established a summer school transition class to offer entering grade 9 students the chance to hone their literacy skills and acquire a credit before they started high school. They also introduced a leadership course for students in upper grades, which coached them in problem-solving, planning and other skills central to creativity. Just as Sakaana's group had envisioned, the staff built a component into the leadership course that required those pupils to work with and develop activities for the transition students. And, consistent with the group's recommendation about developing mastery, Flahat continued to build partnerships for his students with external organizations that could offer them valuable experiences, from The Hospital for Sick Children (SickKids) to the local Scott Mission.

The I-Think program gave Flahat's students a meaningful voice in the running of the school. The experience reflected his belief that "when students are given an opportunity to make a difference—when they have real problems to solve that are connected and related to community and organizations—it ignites a passion for them to engage in their learning."

As students became more engaged, they became more committed; and as they became more committed, they became more successful. The spirit of creativity fostered by the program spread throughout the school, and Flahat began to see his students succeeding in new and unexpected ways. They began winning prizes: SickKids' MedTech Challenge for neurosurgical robotics; the University of Waterloo's Pascal and Fermat Mathematics Contests; the Students for the Advancement of Global Entrepreneurship (SAGE) Canada National Entrepreneurial Competition, Social Enterprise Business category; and even archery competitions. Literacy scores rose. Math scores rose. And the school continues to break ground in its role as a community hub. John Polanyi is now home to one of the city's largest urban gardens, producing over 6,800 kilograms of organic produce while helping students coming out of the youth justice system to acquire new skills. The students also raised money to travel to Nicaragua to build a school, extending their goodwill beyond their own borders. Enrolment has gone up to 800 students, and staff celebrate every student who graduates and goes on to post-secondary education.[*]

Today, the original I-Think team has moved into the background, and the course has been fully incorporated into the school—but the Rotman connection has been maintained, with regular visits to the business school and opportunities for presentations there. Flahat believes that whether individuals realize their dreams depends upon the opportunities afforded them. This idea connects, for him, to the moral purpose of schooling: "As educators we're given the gift to help nurture these dreams. I think it's our responsibility."

---

[*] The board tracks students' graduation and post-secondary education application rates by cohort. John Polanyi has not been operating long enough to report on graduation and post-secondary access rates.

Creativity and the Road to Excellence

Rhodes Scholars are arguably the personification of the "successful" student—accomplished, acclaimed and passionate about learning. In interviewing all but two of the 2015 Rhodes Scholars, Kelly found it striking how many identified the arts specifically, and extracurriculars generally, as being the most valuable components of their schooling. Most of the award recipients believe that these subjects and activities were deeply important to their academic success, sense of community and confidence.

Asked about a formative moment in school, Rhodes Scholar Bernard Soubry described performing a Shakespeare play during his first year as a francophone in an English-speaking high school. "I was still the weird kid who had these twists of language; my syntax wasn't entirely part of the community," he explained. Performance taught Bernard that he was capable of taking risks, receiving constructive feedback and gaining (and, when necessary, feigning) the confidence he needed to grow: "I could pretend to be good at what I was doing, and that was a step towards being able to do it." Performing and "having people respond to me as I wanted them to respond, really cemented the notion that I could be accepted in that community."

Later in their conversation, Kelly asked Bernard what his high school had done to help him excel. He, a model student, believes he flourished most outside the traditional bounds of assessment, when his school invited him to innovate free from the expectation of excellence—when "there wasn't a clear achievement or failure." He was fortunate to have teachers around him "who created an atmosphere where there wasn't a question of achievement, there was a question of creation." One example was his high school economics class, in which he and his classmates were challenged to start a company. Bernard established his own tie-dye business, and it was the process of making his products and finding a market for them that was most meaningful to him, not the excellent mark he received. (That experience also likely refined his business acumen. He spent his early twenties building a bilingual touring theatre company and operating a bakery in Sackville, New Brunswick, and spent the year before attending Oxford as an apprentice carpenter and farmer.)

Caroline Leps, another Rhodes Scholar, spent much of her time in high school with a split focus, juggling schoolwork and competitive musical performance. When Kelly asked how her school had encouraged excellence, Caroline spoke about her commitment to mastering piano and violin, a passion her teachers supported through visible interest as well as flexibility with attendance and assignment deadlines. Caroline, who went on to study international relations and politics, believes that by enabling her to excel both within its walls and beyond, her school bolstered her enthusiasm and achievement. And the visceral experience of playing music and interpreting the work of a composer in her own way fed Caroline's ingenuity, diligence and passion for learning and school.

Caroline has also witnessed passion drive learning in others. A former volunteer at Camp Oochigeas, which serves children with cancer, Caroline remembers the campers' excitement when an activity stirred their interest. Despite the fact that many were ill or in recovery, "when the little ones find something they like, you don't have to encourage them to get going!" Catching frogs, for example, was fun, but was also an opportunity for learning— one the children relished. The counsellors and children would discuss the frogs' habitats, where they slept and if they were male or female. When a school allows children to "find what they are passionate about and run with it, it can foster success in all its students," says Caroline.

For Devin Grant, a Rhodes Scholar who now works in

computer science, the arts were a key part of his personal development. His most formative moment in high school, he says, was when he joined his school choir in grade 9. His experiences in choir marked the end of his shy and introverted childhood. Singing a solo (Frankie Valli's "Can't Take My Eyes Off You") in a choir performance was transformative: "There I was, walking downstage in a white tuxedo with a microphone, blowing kisses at the crowd. It was so drastically different from anything I had ever done before, it really changed how I saw myself." The arts gave Devin a chance to find something he was "good at and comfortable doing," and to strengthen the creative and interpersonal skills that would be so vital to his later success.

These students' recollections reflect a common reality that, often, a student's most formative experiences happen within the context of arts and extracurriculars—exactly the parts of the school program that some write off as the nice-to-haves, not the have-to-haves of a resource-strapped education system—the places where teachers are expected to participate as volunteers outside their formal job descriptions. Yet as we see with these Rhodes Scholars, these are key spaces to seek creative expression, ignite passion and impart invaluable skills. And achievement in the arts can unlock achievement in other domains. As Ken Robinson says, "It's a fundamental human truth that people perform better when they're in touch with things that inspire them."[7] Schools must play a role in nurturing those passions that compel their students to succeed. This has implications both for classrooms and curriculum design, and for the definition of "extra" and "core" activities at school.

Roger Martin's Prosperity Institute has been advising the Ontario government on the importance of developing a "creative economy." Martin has argued that for relatively rich countries like Canada to thrive, it is critical for them to build up a creatively capable population. Innovation, he believes, is the path to prosperity. What with exponential technological growth, we cannot predict what the world will look like in five years, never mind a generation. Creativity and critical thinking—the kinds of integrative thinking promoted by curricula like I-Think—need to be cultivated in our students so that they can adapt to a world running and changing at an unprecedented speed.

Schools too often focus on skills that are easily measured. While creativity is difficult to assess, it is nevertheless an essential skill and must become a greater focus of any classroom that hopes to prepare students for the realities of life in the twenty-first century. Creativity opens students' minds to possibilities, fosters new ideas and solutions, develops perseverance and risk-taking, and taps into and fuels passions. According to Rhodes Scholar Bernard, the ideal school environment is one in which "questions are necessary and creativity encouraged."

THREE

SOCIAL-EMOTIONAL LEARNING

"If you care about academic performance, you need to care about more than academic performance."

—ROGER WEISSBERG
of the Collaborative on Academic,
Social and Emotional Learning[1]

When we asked our cohort of Rhodes Scholars to reveal the most important things they learned in school, their answers were surprising, yet similar. They didn't list math or history or literature, but rather a range of non-cognitive skills that sustained them through their education.

Rhodes Scholar Benjamin Mappin-Kasirer identified "time management" as his most valuable takeaway from school. In the middle of high school, he fell in love with fencing, competing at the national level. Suddenly, he was practising for hours, five days a week—yet remarkably, his grades started going up and up and up. In fact, he did better in school during the fencing season than in the off times. The more Benjamin had on his plate, the more efficient he was in completing his work. Unfazed by the pressure, his philosophy soon became "the more you do, the more time you have."

One of the social skills Benjamin learned that helped him succeed when he took on new challenges was asking for help when he needed it. He never appreciated just how powerful a tool this is until he began volunteering as a tutor in a low-income school in New Haven while he was studying literature at Yale. He was surprised, there, to realize that the kids who were already doing the best were the first ones in line for after-school tutoring. The children who were really struggling were much more reluctant to reach out. Despite its large class sizes and limited resources, this school did have teachers and programs available to those who needed support, but as Benjamin observed, "often the challenge isn't finding the help, it's asking for it." Benjamin was lucky to have understood from a young age that seeking assistance is a practice of success, and not an indicator of failure. For most children, this insight is not intuitive—it is one of a number of lessons they should learn at home and school, but often don't.

Social-Emotional Skills and Schools

Thriving under pressure, seeking help when you need it—these lessons are rarely integrated explicitly into the curriculum, but educational researchers view these and other social-emotional skills as vital to students' success. In the 1980s, the U.S. Collaborative on Academic, Social, and Emotional Learning (CASEL) identified five "non-cognitive" competencies that are now widely accepted as crucial to emotional development and well-being: self-awareness, self-management, social awareness, relationship skills and responsible decision making.[2] In life and in work, students need to be able to identify and manage their feelings and behaviours, understand the perspectives of others, form and maintain a range of relationships, and make decisions that are considerate of consequences and of others' needs.

Skills like these not only help to sustain children emotionally during the stresses of schooling but prime them for emotional stability and professional success later in life. Employer and business groups consistently report that the skills they most seek in employees are non-cognitive, like teamwork, strong communication and self-management.[3] In the 1970s, the Marxist economist/sociologist duo Samuel Bowles and Herbert Gintis used school and labour force data to show that, relative to those demonstrating intelligence and critical thinking, it was gradu- ates with traits like docility, dependability and persistence who achieved higher earnings and levels of employment.[4] And Nobel Prize–winning economist James Heckman and colleagues used a national U.S. dataset to reveal that social-emotional skills have an impact on long-term achievement and behaviour that is either equal to or greater than the impact of intellectual skills; when their participants' social-emotional skills improved, they were more likely to stay in school; earn more; and avoid tobacco, marijuana and criminal behaviour.[5*]

Despite these findings, these valuable non-cognitive quali- ties are often dismissively termed "soft skills," and traditionally have not been considered an educational priority. School systems emphasize *academic* achievement as the main "outcome" of edu- cation, and measure their success primarily in test scores. To give just one example, in a massive international study on what a teacher's role should be, the OECD makes no reference to work in the social-emotional domain—the work of supporting chil- dren's physical and mental well-being and helping them to build and maintain relationships, attentiveness and responsiveness.[6]

Families have been expected to support and nourish their children's emotional growth on their own—and some insist this tradition should be maintained. In the influential education tome *Promoting Social and Emotional Learning: Guidelines for Educators,*

---

* In another large-scale study, Heckman's team demonstrated that individuals who achieved a GED, a high school equivalency diploma, had earnings that aligned with those of dropouts and *not* with high school graduates, despite comparable test-score achievement. They hypothesized that people who graduate from high school generally have stronger social-emotional skills than those with GEDs—and social-emotional skills are more valuable to employers than cognitive achievement alone.

Maurice J. Elias wrote about the challenge of overcoming the notion that "the family should be the place where the child learns to understand, control and work through emotions; social and emotional issues are essentially private concerns that should be left at the door when a child enters a school."[7]

The notion that social-emotional education be confined to the home, however, may not be in our children's best interest. Right now, large-scale data points to record-breaking levels of social and emotional challenges in children and adolescents. In 2011–2012, the Toronto District School Board surveyed over 100,000 students in grades 7–12 about emotional well-being, among other issues. The results, particularly for students in secondary school, are disconcerting. Thirty-four percent of students in grades 9–12 reported that they were nervous or anxious "all of the time" or "often," and 38 percent said they were under a lot of stress. One in five felt that they were losing confidence in themselves or that they were unable to overcome difficulties. Three quarters worried about school—and their futures.[8] Students with poor emotional well-being are less likely to feel comfortable asking for help; they have fewer friends and are almost three times as likely to report being bullied or excluded.[*]

Data also suggests that parents want help. A recent analysis of 11,171 grants awarded to parent-led school councils across Ontario shows that councils most frequently seek funding to

---

[*] Students' social and emotional struggles do not appear to be correlated to their parents' income, education or marital status. Students' own academic performance is another poor indicator—an accomplished child is not necessarily a happy one. The highest achieving group of students, Asian girls, are also the most likely to report emotional problems. Despite their achievements, high-performing students with social and emotional challenges are much less likely to believe in their own success: only 48 percent think they are making good progress in school, whereas 73 percent of students who have strong social-emotional skills feel they are succeeding.

support activities that promote student mental health and well-being and improved parent–child communication.[9]*

In the face of rising mental health challenges among children, the education system must expand its focus to nurture the whole child. Large-scale research shows that social-emotional skills can be taught, and that when schools are successful at doing so, it can be transformative for children.[10] Select schools have begun to prioritize social-emotional learning (SEL), and a meta-analysis of these programs reveals that they dramatically improve children's social-emotional skills, like reading emotional cues, resolving conflicts, setting goals and making decisions. SEL programs have also been shown to have strong positive effects on students' attitudes toward themselves and others, reducing behavioural problems and self-reported emotional distress.[11]

One of the most unexpected findings of the meta-analysis is one of its most significant: SEL programs do not merely impact behaviour; they are also correlated to higher academic performance. Students who completed SEL programs outperformed their peers by 11 percent in their grades and test scores. With its two key messages—high-quality SEL programs improve learning and positively affect how kids feel and relate to each other—this meta-analysis has helped to shape the conversation about the role schools can and should play in children's emotional lives.

Within Canada, many schools are already choosing to place emphasis on the importance of non-cognitive skills, building SEL into their curricula and establishing mental health, anti-bullying and community-building initiatives. These schools of

---

* Forty-four percent of the grants went to fund these areas, compared to 27 percent to fund projects relating to home-based learning (e.g., literacy or math nights), 12 percent for improving access (e.g., website development or translation) and 11 percent for boosting family–school connections generally (e.g., network development, parent surveys).

the future are providing their students with a well of emotional resources that will support them in their personal lives and professional careers, and can serve as a model for our education system as a whole.

Six-year-old Mohammed was new to George Webster, having attended a kindergarten program for students with disabilities at a nearby school the previous year—and new to Canada, only recently emigrated from Somalia. Alongside seven other classmates, Mohammed was enrolled in a grade 1 class for children with multiple exceptionalities. The class shared a special education teacher, an educational assistant and a variety of other helpers, including special needs assistants and parent volunteers. Despite the high adult-to-student ratio, addressing the students' complex needs kept the staff on their toes.

Mohammed was thought to have a developmental disability that placed him in the lowest percentile for intelligence, according to psychoeducational testing. These results were complicated, however, by the fact that Mohammed had autism, and had difficulty communicating his thoughts and desires. In class, his behaviour was unpredictable. At times, he complied happily with classroom expectations, sitting quietly at circle time, playing co-operatively in small groups or obediently eating a snack. Mohammed, however, could be a runner. When he was confronted with the unfamiliar, challenged by a transition or unable to express his thoughts and feelings in words, he would often run away. These episodes were sudden and frequent. At recess, for example, he would be playing on the playground one moment and running from the school grounds the next. Teachers spent a good chunk of Mohammed's first year at George Webster chasing after him.

Even before he had finished grade 1, the grade 2 teacher, Jason James, and the educational assistant, Debbie Grounds, had begun to study Mohammed to understand what conditions were necessary for his success. James had noticed Mohammed's astonishing ability to read and memorize, despite his struggles to articulate his own thoughts. He began to steal a few minutes to pop downstairs from his classroom to read with Mohammed. Mohammed was always deeply interested in books and enjoyed listening to James read, occasionally joining in by reciting familiar phrases. While it was not clear how much Mohammed understood, James had clearly identified a passion and strength of his future student that would be worth developing further. James explained, "Mohammed had tools, but didn't know how to use them."

When Mohammed finally started grade 2, Grounds knew that the first step was to build a relationship with him. Aware of his passion for cars, Grounds set up an area in the classroom that she called the "Pit Stop," where characters from the movie *Cars* were depicted sharing positive affirmations like "I can stay in the race" and "I'm on the right track." She also created a five-point scale that allowed Mohammed to better express how he was feeling— from Level 1, calm and ready to race, to Level 5, angry and with a blown tire. Over time, Mohammed began to comment, "If I blow a tire, it's no big deal, I can go to the Pit Stop." Grounds also taught him that going for a walk, reading a book and taking deep breaths could help him to reset.

Grounds and James began to use Mohammed's love of books to teach him to identify and accept his own feelings. As Mohammed demonstrated different feelings, they would share examples of characters having the same experiences to help him put names to his feelings and show him how universal they are. And using a technique called "social stories," the team helped Mohammed learn appropriate language for common social situations. Through role plays, coaching and ongoing feedback, Mohammed began to feel more comfortable going "off script."

One day, Grounds noticed Mohammed watching the other children on the playground during recess (his class was confined to a more structured play area). She and James agreed that, with support, Mohammed was ready to join the mainstream group at recess. Grounds asked Mohammed how he felt about this idea, and he admitted that he was scared. Together, they found a tree to sit under in the big yard and read a book about being scared. Grounds reassured him that she gets scared too when she tries something new. They repeated this process several times, always under the same tree. One day, Mohammed didn't want to read the "scared" book—he wanted the "proud" book. Grounds told him she was proud of him, too. From then on, they began to interact with others in the yard. When Grounds saw Mohammed watching others intently, they would approach together and ask if he could play too. He did not always stay with group activities for a long time, but he began to give them a try. Over time, Mohammed was able to be with the mainstream students during recess without much extra supervision.

Grounds and James knew that in order to set Mohammed up for success, they had to improve his self-confidence. Grounds said, "We focused on what he *could* do, and once he had built confidence in that, he was more willing to try new things." But building confidence, like all social-emotional skill development, is not a straightforward or simple matter. Boosting Mohammed's autonomy and assurance first involved forming strong bonds of trust with him, as well as teaching him how to make mistakes and persist through them.

When the class was preparing a play for the Winter Concert, James and Grounds thought that Mohammed would be a great narrator, but were aware he might be afraid to perform live. As a backup plan, they created a videotape of him narrating the story. They were right on both counts. Mohammed did do a great job of narrating the concert—on video—but at the prospect of performing live, he had a meltdown, trashing his classroom in the process. As he panicked, Grounds put on calming music, and told him, "You know what, I would be scared, too." Mohammed turned to her and said, "Hug." They played the recording rather than forcing Mohammed to perform—and the video later became a source of pride and delight for Mohammed, as he saw what he could do. James commented, "What I've learned from children like Mohammed—I am now more conscious of making other people feel comfortable so they can be themselves."

By encouraging Mohammed to take a big risk and by supporting him when he was unsuccessful, James and Grounds strengthened their bond with their student. Challenge and risk-taking are particularly important in special education settings, where students often face worse outcomes than do students of similar levels of disability in integrated settings.[12] James and Grounds carefully planned their learning activities so that their students could take manageable risks and fail safely.

Five years later, Mohammed was able to articulate his reality in his own words:

I'm Mohammed and I'm 10 years old. I would like you to know some things about me.

I am curious, friendly, imaginative and an amazing reader. There are many things that I think are fun and that I am really good at doing. One of the things I'm really good at is listening to bugs.

There are also things that are hard for me to learn. Some of my friends are good at these things and I wish I were too.

One thing that I think is hard is to think and to make decisions on my own. When I can't do that I feel blue.

I get confused at some things that might not make other people confused. One thing that sometimes makes me feel confused is when people talk. It is sometimes hard for me to understand what you are saying or what you are asking me. Because I am an amazing reader, it is sometimes easier for me to understand what you are saying or asking me when I see things are written.

I want to understand and sometimes even look at your face to try and find the answer. I try to remember to use my brain and when I don't know the answer, say "I don't know."

I learn a lot from looking at my friends. But sometimes when I copy them too much, they feel sad. I need to try to remember it's OK to look at my friends for help, but not to copy everything that they do or say.

I notice that people act differently when they are upset. Some people like to be quiet and alone. Others want to be around friends. When I'm upset, I usually cry, stomp, yell, laugh, kick and feel like I want to knock the trees down.

But, I want to be included just like everyone. I may be different, but I'm a boy too.

Mohammed created this text for a bulletin board designed to teach the rest of the school about autism. When she saw it, Nancy had to confront her initial assumptions about his capabilities; she had underestimated Mohammed. Fortunately, the educators who worked with him most closely had not.

Self-Regulation
Lianne McBride is a grade 5 teacher at Cindrich School in Surrey, British Columbia, and a leader in bringing SEL into the classroom.

Her journey began when she learned about the importance of self-regulation, which is the emotional process by which one identifies factors causing stress, reduces them and returns to a calm and alert state. Self-regulation is foundational to the development of other social-emotional competencies and to overall wellness.

McBride encountered the concept at a summer seminar hosted by the Surrey School Board in 2010. The keynote speaker was Dr. Stuart Shanker, the author of *Calm, Alert, and Learning*, who spoke convincingly about how the skill could be taught and how it could revolutionize learning. "It was like a light bulb going off in my head, a life-changing moment," said McBride. A devoted teacher with twenty years of experience, McBride had been growing increasingly frustrated at school. About 90 percent of her students were new immigrants whose first languages ranged from Urdu to Punjabi to Spanish. Many entered school with "huge, complex needs," whether they had fled conflict in their home countries, had experienced gaps in their learning due to inter-rupted schooling, were struggling to communicate in English, had special education needs or had missed breakfast. These needs were layered upon the ten-year-old students' classic pre-teen anxieties about friendships and fitting in.

McBride was discouraged by her students' behaviour—by how frequently they acted out and lost focus. "School would start at 8:30 in the morning and by a quarter to nine I felt like I was a repeating record giving them directions on what to do, how to sit down, how to hang up their coats, and start their work. Every day I felt like I was being negative and reactive," she said. The experience was exhausting, and her efforts to control her class produced only short-term results. Whatever correction or strat-egy she tried, "the next day, the behaviours would still be there."

After hearing Shanker talk about self-regulation, McBride gladly signed up to be part of a new inquiry-based project her board was spearheading to help kids learn to recognize and manage stress. The project meant working with a group of teachers from six schools across the board and social emotional coordinator Taunya Shaw. Shaw was a specialist in assessment and counselling, newly appointed to lead and support the board's efforts to promote SEL. Shaw was excited to take on the role and inspired by the challenges it posed. "Social-emotional learning is quite unique," she said, "We expect kids to come to school with these skills in place, yet we're not seeing that."

Starting in January 2011, McBride began the new SEL program by breaking down the key concepts of self-regulation for her students. Using an engine metaphor for illustration, McBride taught them to recognize when their engines were running "high" (feeling hyper and unfocused) or "low" (feeling sluggish or dejected).* McBride now starts every day with an "engine check," in which each student is asked to place a popsicle stick in one of three jars, labelled "High," "Low" and "Just right." The class then gathers to discuss why they put their sticks where they did, helping students learn to recognize their emotional states, and creating an environment in which feeling and sharing is encouraged.

McBride has a poster pinned to her classroom wall that lists strategies to try if your engine is running high or low. For high engines, the poster recommends grabbing earmuffs to shut out distractions, drinking water, pulling on an exercise band—even going for a quick run in the enclosed courtyard outside the classroom. In an interview with *The Vancouver Sun*, Shaw revealed that, despite early reservations about letting students leave the classroom, "The results were astounding. The kids absolutely

---

* This terminology comes from the Alert Program's book, *How Does Your Engine Run?*, which teaches kids and parents to identify and then change their levels of arousal.

loved it. When they come back to their desks, they are more focused and they're not asking to leave to go to the bathroom four or five more times."[13] When students' engines run low, strategies might include alleviating hunger with a snack, doing jumping jacks for an energy boost, or engaging in a blast of creativity with some playdough.

At the beginning of the school year, before she had brought self-regulation techniques into the classroom, McBride had asked her students what they needed in order to be good learners. The students had created "learning toolboxes," in which they detailed the factors that helped them focus each day: a good breakfast, a break, exercise. Daman could not think of anything to write.

Daman was one of McBride's most challenging students. He had no specific learning impediments and his English was relatively strong, but he struggled in school in more ways than one. McBride would often take a minute to speak to him one-to-one in the mornings, asking him about his sleep the night before, if he had eaten and what he was going to do to get ready to learn. Daman would shrug, say he didn't know, or make eye contact with a buddy as he giggled. He frequently disrupted McBride's lessons by sticking out his tongue or rolling his eyes. He never finished his assignments. During his first oral presentation, he simply held a paper up in front of his face and laughed. At recess and lunch, day after day, he would find himself in some kind of trouble, but could not recognize his own role in any of the problems. He would say, "I was just playing basketball and this guy came up and hit me." He never acknowledged that having thrown a ball at another child's head, for example, had provoked the fight.

When Kelly spoke with Stuart Shanker he talked about the importance of overcoming the notion that "some children are born bad, that they have some sort of a gene that predisposes them to trouble." Self-regulation work emphasizes the impact of stress on children's behaviour, and encourages teachers, faced with challenging students, to ask: *What is it in the child that makes him/her so easily overstressed? Is the way I respond to this child's behaviour contributing to making things better or worse?* With an attitude rooted in patient investigation, Shanker believes you can always change a child's trajectory, no matter the severity of their behavioural problems. A key method is to find ways to encourage the child to *want* to take part in more desirable social interactions.

A few months after she started teaching her students how to self-regulate, McBride began to see some progress. Daman came to school one morning and (perhaps because some of his friends were absent) simply hung up his bag, sat down at his desk and began to work. For the very first time, he completed an assigned task. At the end of the lesson, McBride praised Daman, and he beamed. She asked him what had put him into a frame of mind to get work done, and he wagered an answer: he had had a good sleep and was at school before the bell. "I really made a big deal of it," recalled McBride, even sending him down to the principal's office to celebrate. Slowly, small successes like this one began to mount. Daman learned to better articulate his needs, and McBride secured him a pair of headphones and a disk cushion to help address the hypersensitivity that fuelled his attention issues.

By the school year's end, Daman's ability to understand the consequences of his actions had increased dramatically. In late May, after sneaking into a classroom and stealing a granola bar, he took responsibility for his actions. "My engine's really not working," he told McBride. "I totally made a mistake there. I shouldn't have done it and I won't do it again." This was significant progress for a child who had not previously admitted to any wrongdoing.

Progress was evident in his schoolwork, too. In May, there was a school-wide "speech fest," and Daman was the first child to volunteer for the opportunity to present. In a speech that could not have been more dissimilar to his first of the year, Daman was clear and poised. Writing about the experience afterwards, he said, "I liked my speech topic because it was hard. The hard part was to find information about lung cancer, like how do people get lung cancer. I am proud of my speech topic and how I said my speech." When asked to reflect upon his learning needs, Daman wrote that he had discovered that year that he needed to be calm and alert to work at his full potential.

Daman's mother observed the difference, too. She and McBride had met several times over the school year, and it was clear that education was very important in the family. She was anxious that Daman succeed, but she didn't have a good read on how he was doing or what supports he needed. She often asked, "Is he going to be okay?" but did not always seem ready for an honest answer. Her own stress was interfering with her ability to hear what McBride was telling her. When they met in the early spring, she cried as McBride reviewed the turnaround she had witnessed: Daman's new success at recess and lunch, his improved communication skills, the positive effect the headphones and disk cushion had made on his ability to focus. When she saw the efforts supporting her son's progress, she became motivated to improve conditions at home, too, working harder to get Daman to bed and to school on time.

SEL will always be a complement to what is going on in the home, good or bad. Coping with poverty or disruptive life changes deeply affects students' whole lives, including life at school, but an alliance between parents and teachers to nurture children's social-emotional needs can help to alleviate stressors. McBride often partners with parents to improve their children's well-being. In one striking example, she worked with the mother of a student named Naaz to help him cope with his anxiety. McBride and Naaz's mother had been in frequent communication, and both were concerned about him. He displayed high levels of anxiety and was not thriving academically. When McBride asked Naaz to deliver a message to another teacher two doors down the hall, he had a debilitating panic attack on the way. He fled to the bathroom, and it took two teachers to ease him back into the classroom. When McBride tried to talk with him the next day, he acted like nothing had happened. Naaz consistently refused to acknowledge that his anxiety existed—and that it was a problem.

With keen support from his mother, McBride began to teach Naaz to recognize signs of anxiety—to know that if his heart was racing, breath short, or face flushed, it was a sign that his body was stressed. She also gave him direct instructions on ways to calm down: take deep breaths, get a glass of water, ask an adult or friend for help. These coping strategies, and McBride's and his mother's support, helped him to manage his anxiety and to see that it is neither shameful nor unconquerable. By the end of the year, Naaz was able to acknowledge in writing, "I experience stress, and it's OK." This recognition felt to McBride and his mother like a major step forward.

SEL has completely reframed McBride's teaching, and become the "#1 thing" she emphasizes with her students. It has helped her to stop "being a reactive teacher, putting out fires, blaming parents" and given her the tools to be a proactive one. The work she does is neither social work nor counselling—it is recognizably teaching, with explicit learning goals, planned activities and dedicated class time designed to meet her students' learning needs. Research has shown that the most effective SEL programs are delivered by teachers in their own classrooms, rather than by specialized external providers;[14] McBride's capacity to work with her students on these core social-emotional lessons, day after day, over the course of the school year, enabled her students' progress.

How we feel and our relationship patterns often seem like fundamental parts of ourselves, the direct and immovable result of some cocktail of nature and nurture. McBride's story is just one example of something a bit counterintuitive—that social-emotional skills can be taught. The learning that goes on in McBride's classroom is powerful, and happily, it is not as unique as you might think.

Growth Mindset

Self-regulation is not the only social-emotional skill that has a strong impact on achievement. Professor Carol Dweck, an experimental psychologist at Columbia University, has used evidence from classroom experiments and brain imaging research to show that when people adopt "growth mindsets"—when they believe that their abilities can improve through dedication and hard work—they are significantly more likely to progress.[15] She and her team are building up a base of research that shows that simple interventions can effectively reshape students' mindsets. One such strategy involves carefully cultivating the messages we impart to children about their own abilities. Telling them that they cannot succeed—either explicitly or implicitly—can be destructive. Interestingly, so can praising them for their intelligence. Dweck's research reveals that children are most motivated to learn and achieve when their efforts are praised, rather than their smarts or talents—praising the latter can reinforce children's complacency and reduce their drive. Increasingly, schools are using these findings to teach their students to build growth mindsets that will nourish them on their paths to success.

Developing its students' growth mindsets is a priority at Granite Ridge Education Centre (GREC). A brand-new, modern kindergarten-to-grade-12 public school, GREC brings together four hundred students from various small communities outside Kingston, Ontario. Across grades and subjects, GREC emphasizes the development of attitudes and social-emotional skills that have been linked to long-term success. One way in which the school has sought to improve its students' growth mindsets is by stepping back from streaming.

Streaming is the common educational practice of separating students into different courses (with different materials and different methods) on the basis of their perceived abilities or presumed career paths. In Ontario secondary schools, grade 9 and 10 math, English, science, geography, history and French courses are offered in two versions, applied and academic. The academic curriculum is described as theoretical and abstract, whereas the applied curriculum is intended to be "hands-on," structured to prepare students for college or the workplace (instead of university). The labels "applied" and "academic" are intended to be value neutral, but the programs produce distinctly unequal outcomes.

GREC principal Heather Highet is a dynamic educator who recently completed a Master's in Educational Leadership, studying large-scale international and Canadian research on the adverse effects of streaming. She learned that poor and marginalized students are disproportionately assigned to vocational streams, like applied math, and that vocational streams consistently depress the achievement of their students.[16] Across Ontario, on provincial assessments of math and literacy, students in applied courses scored 40 percent lower than those in academic courses—despite the fact that the exams were tailored to each stream. Students in vocational streams receive not only a limited curriculum and less exposure to peers who are succeeding, but also a discouraging message about their abilities. By placing a cap on how much students can learn, vocational streams implicitly communicate to students that their abilities are both lesser and fixed—a message detrimental toward the development of a healthy growth mindset.[17]

Armed with this knowledge, Highet and her staff decided to try an experiment. GREC launched a pilot project to destream grade 9 math, so that all students would be required to learn the same curriculum together. Their goal was to raise their expectations for their students and encourage them to achieve more than they had previously been told was possible. If, after one semester, any students were unhappy, they would have the option to switch back to an applied stream. To ensure students in the newly destreamed math program received the necessary supports, the school created a learning strategies elective that taught students how to develop their study and organizational skills. The course also taught them explicitly about growth mindsets and how to develop their own. One third of the grade 9s signed up for the learning strategies course, including a student named Connie, who struggles with dyslexia.

In most Ontario schools, Connie likely would have been steered toward applied math. She says she was "pretty nervous" when she began the destreamed course; she had struggled with math after grade 6, and she wasn't sure how her dyslexia would affect her chances of success. The learning strategies course helped to reassure her. She remembers exploring Carol Dweck's *Mindset Works* website, watching videos on the workings of the brain, and learning how to "hear your fixed mindset voice" and avoid traps like telling yourself you are incapable.

She was surprised to discover that she enjoyed her destreamed course. Her teacher, Mike Smith, reworked the curriculum to provide both hands-on learning experiences *and* the chance to build theory from them. For example, his students dropped balls of different sizes from the school's second storey, first predicting then measuring the height of the bounces. They then used the data they collected to construct equations. Connie admitted she initially found the course challenging, but soon realized: "I could do it." Newly inspired, Connie signed up for academic math again in grade 10. Now that she was "no longer intimidated," she realized she genuinely enjoyed the subject.

In the first year, not one student switched out of the new math course. When the students took the provincial academic math exam at the end of the year, 89 percent of them met or exceeded the provincial standard (a level 3, or B grade)—a percentage that exceeded the provincial and school district average. Highet was thrilled with this result. Among the students who were successful on the provincial test, 59 percent had been *below* the provincial standard in the previous round of provincial testing (in grade 6). The new test scores represented a leap in achievement and a change in attitude. "What stood out," Highet said, "was the students understood that they really have to work at something and not give up. Students told me that it is cool to know that a person is not fixed in intelligence."[18]

In the second year of the program, GREC students continued to outperform the rest of the board and province in math, but challenges arose. Six students, most of whom had significant learning difficulties, opted to switch to applied math in January. Without universal involvement among the students, Mike Smith was forced to carry the extra burden of teaching two groups of students in the same class differently. Dissatisfaction, too, began to mount among some parents and teachers, who were frustrated that students had to choose between taking learning strategies or French—many believed that math was being privileged above other subjects. Reluctantly, in its third year, Highet halted the destreamed program, and GREC went back to offering applied and academic math in every grade.

The school has made some permanent changes to its math program, however, that are designed to structurally reinforce students' growth mindset. All grade 9 students now begin math together for one month, during which they are taught math concepts and learning skills, including lessons on developing confidence and overcoming negative thoughts. All students, including those who have experienced difficulties with the subject, are now actively counselled to consider taking academic math, and math classes have been timetabled to make it easy to switch streams—especially to switch "up" into the academic stream, which is rare in Ontario. There has been significant collaboration between teachers in the applied and academic streams, and they have developed shared learning goals for all students. Mike Smith says his teaching has changed permanently. He now integrates what he would have described as "applied" approaches with more abstract learning in his courses. Highet says she is most proud when she sees kids who are really struggling with math, literacy and behaviour exercising their growth mindsets and pushing through their difficulties toward success.

Children are reluctant to take on challenges without significant encouragement and support, and too many schools limit their students' success through either explicit messages or signals like streaming. GREC demonstrates that by dismantling these messages, and teaching kids how to employ their own mindsets to work *for* them, it is possible to open up higher plains of learning for all students.

At the same time, it is important not to turn these powerful SEL tools into a "silver bullet" that replaces the need for a full range of adequate social supports. A few public voices have exploited

Dweck's findings on growth mindsets, arguing that they show that systematic inequality is no excuse for poor academic performance. In 2014, a reporter in *National Geographic* wrote,

> Blaming teachers, class size, lack of money, family conditions, and other "situational" factors . . . have increasingly over the past century let the student off the hook and turned underperformers into victims of circumstance rather than creators of opportunity. The new direction [in education emphasizing growth mindsets] aims to empower children with a sense of personal responsibility and free will.[19]

And describing Dweck's research, journalists in *The Atlantic* argued, "We may not have to eradicate poverty" to improve students' success.[20] These arguments inflate the potential of growth mindsets to dismantle the effects of poverty and racism, and ultimately let the system off the hook. As Dweck and her colleagues wrote in a response to the *Atlantic* article, "Mindset interventions are not a replacement for addressing root problems in schools or society, such as poor teaching or the widespread and brutal effects of poverty and bias." The scientists emphasized the fundamental importance of safety, security and adequate resources at home and at school to children's well-being and success. Thoughtful and well-tested psychological interventions have the potential to *support* student success, not create it.[21]

Stop Now and Plan

At Nancy's former school, George Webster, an SEL program called snap became a vital resource for supporting student success. Before Nancy's arrival at George Webster in 2008, a "Start Right" program had already been initiated there. Once a week,

Jimmy Madeira, a youth worker with a local children's mental health agency, would engage a small group of kindergarten students in activities that helped them develop the social skills their teachers found they were lacking. Playing with Madeira, they learned to take turns, to help each other out and to stay calm when things went wrong. Madeira was so effective with the kids that staff began pulling him into meetings with students. It was through Madeira that the school was introduced to SNAP, which could provide support for older students.

SNAP, or Stop Now And Plan, teaches students how to calm themselves down and make good choices in situations that could lead to aggression. Developed by Dr. Leena Augimeri, who heads up the program at the Child Development Institute (CDI), SNAP was first inspired by Augimeri's own family dynamics. She has three brothers and knew first hand that you can have "three boys from the same family—one will be fine, one may get into trouble but get back on track and the third may experience major issues such as involvement with the criminal justice system." Augimeri wanted to understand why this was the case, and what types of intervention might disrupt the progression of destructive behaviour. SNAP, the result of her decades of research, employs cognitive behavioural therapy (CBT) techniques to alter patterns of thought and behaviour that are hindering a child, and engages the family, school and community for support. Random control trials show that SNAP-treated children demonstrate significant improvement in behaviour compared to an attention-only (placebo) control group, with their treatment gains maintained over time.[22] Brain imaging research conducted at SickKids Hospital and the University of Toronto also reveals that successful treatment with SNAP produces substantial changes in the brain systems responsible for cognitive control and self-regulation.[23] Some of the program's former participants credit it with having saved their lives.

In 2010, George Webster Elementary joined CDI's school-based SNAP program. With the institute's help, the George Webster team committed to implementing the full SNAP program with all grade 3 students, providing younger children with an introduction and older students with a review, and employing SNAP principles as an essential, whole-school approach to conflict resolution.

In the fall term, Rolando Carrillo, a child and youth worker, came to the school to launch the program. He taught all of the students and their teachers key tenets of SNAP. The kids learned to pay attention to how they were feeling in any given moment, and to use their body's physiological signs as warnings. When their breath sped up, their faces flushed or their fists clenched, the students were taught that they should stop and take some deep breaths, count backwards from ten, put their hands in their pockets and tell themselves things like "I don't want to get in trouble."

Grade 3 was where the real learning happened. George Webster's grade 3 class was selected to pilot the program, and was given twelve weeks of SNAP training. The endlessly patient Carrillo conducted twelve one-hour workshops, each with a different theme—friendship, bullying, following rules—that layered onto the lessons of the last. Carrillo would ask the students to describe real conflicts that occurred in the classroom or on the playground, and then he would have them practise strategies for calming down. Together, they created plans to make the problems smaller. If someone didn't want to let you play, you could ask again nicely, find another group to play with, solicit a teacher's help, snap your fingers to detract from the urge to hit, or simply walk away from the situation without engaging the other student at all.

Carrillo would film the students while they role-played, and then show them the footage in the following class, giving them an opportunity to reflect on their strategies and to offer constructive feedback. Students loved seeing themselves on the big screen and giving each other tips: "Remember to put your hands in your pocket!", "Turn around and walk away!", "Good job getting help from an adult!"

The teachers began to incorporate SNAP into their dealings with students. If they saw someone getting agitated, they would ask, "How are you feeling? What can you do?" Ken Dewey, one of the grade 3 teachers, remembers the idea of choice being eye-opening for the kids. When they responded to a conflict, they were *choosing* to make the problem bigger or smaller. Students began to head off problems by taking a break, going to get a drink of water or reflecting before reacting. SNAP soon became a kind of mantra when students were faced with social challenges, and they learned to use its techniques to approach problems, examine their underlying issues and respond appropriately.

Years later, George Webster is still a SNAP school, and Carrillo is still there. SNAP is currently being used in more than fifteen school boards across Canada, and has begun to spread throughout the world.

Growing a System

Cindrich, GREC, George Webster and many other schools across Canada are beginning to adopt SEL programs into their curricula. This "one school, one classroom at a time" work is important, but in order to be really effective, it needs a system behind it. Only governments have the tools and structures to ensure that SEL is prioritized in every school across the province, and that all schools have access to high-quality resources to inform their practices.

This is not an easy task, but it is possible. Spurred on by tragedy, British Columbia's government, school boards, faculties of education and teachers have been working to build a system around SEL for the last twenty years. In 1997, a fourteen-year-old South Asian Canadian girl named Reena Virk, long bullied and excluded at school, was beaten and murdered by her classmates. Her murder sparked an outpouring of grief and outrage, and began a larger conversation about children being more vulnerable than we know, or want to believe. The Columbine school shooting in the United States in 1999 further fuelled the conversation,[24] and a year and a half later, two fourteen-year-olds in B.C., Hamed Nastoh in Surrey, and Dawn-Marie Wesley in Mission, committed suicide, each citing bullying as a cause. Their suicide notes made it clear that these vulnerable children had not seen their schools as places to which they could turn for help.

Shelley Hymel, a psychologist at the University of British Columbia who has been instrumental in the development of SEL in B.C., remembers that time as a "perfect storm—schools were worried, kids were dying." Public outcry and professional concern led to an infusion of research and resources around bullying and violence prevention. A key part of the response was to frame schools' work around positive approaches to supporting children's well-being and overall social development. Alongside the development of new interventions, the government decided to change its accountability system. After a two-year consultation process, the government introduced the B.C. performance standards for social responsibility in 2001.[25]

The performance standards were initially an optional framework that schools could implement to encourage their students to develop social responsibility and other social-emotional skills. The framework emphasized four strands of social action: contributing to classroom and school communities; solving problems in peaceful ways; valuing diversity and defending human rights; and exercising democratic rights and responsibilities. Someone who was exceeding expectations "considered others' views and used some effective strategies for resolving minor conflicts; took responsibility and showed good judgment about when to get adult help" and "could explain an increasing variety of problems or issues and generate and evaluate strategies."

When the standards were adopted, Lisa Pedrini was a brand-new safe schools coordinator for the Vancouver School Board, and remembers a distinctly positive buzz: "Teachers weren't obligated to use them, but there was a good deal of interest in them from the beginning. The standards really started conversations— How do we teach this? What do we have to do as adults to make sure we're modelling it? How do we make it clear this is valued in our schools?"

Almost immediately after the standards were introduced, there was a change of provincial government. The new Liberal government kept the social responsibility standards but added a more stringent accountability layer. Teachers were now required to report at least once a year on students' progress in these areas. According to Hymel, the reporting requirement had the effect of spurring research and prompting educators to take students' social and emotional development more seriously. "Schools had to be accountable," she said. "In B.C. schools, social and moral development was now part of education. Some people said that was more rhetoric than implementation, but with accountability that began to shift."

In B.C.'s sixty school districts, teachers were responsible for turning this high-minded provincial policy into concrete action. Pedrini, who was in charge of implementing new strategies for the Vancouver School Board, remembers frustration in this period. Teachers were questioning how to juggle the work involved in teaching social responsibility with the continuing pressure to teach the basics. Some of them asked, "Why is this our job?" Pedrini often found herself reminding crowds of teachers at professional development workshops that schools and teachers fundamentally *want* to "develop whole people who can learn in the world." The Ministry of Education had defined social responsibility as a shared responsibility, part of which belonged to schools. And Pedrini drew on testimonials from the many educators who found that time spent "figuring out how to get along together, especially at the beginning" would allow classes to progress faster as the year went on.

Initially, Pedrini found that teachers in inner-city schools were more receptive to teaching social responsibility. They, like the George Webster staff, already saw supporting students' social competencies as a part of their job, and they were interested in acquiring better tools. Schools in more affluent neighbourhoods were initially less convinced about the importance of the work, and their teachers were more concerned about being held to account for taking time "away" from academics. For this reason, when the Vancouver School Board launched a pilot project in conjunction with UBC researchers, called MindUP, they selected four enthusiastic inner-city schools to test out the program. MindUP was designed to provide students with strategies to help them focus, reduce stress and work together more effectively.

Some of the educators at these four schools were nonetheless skeptical. One grade 6 teacher rolled her eyes during her training, and said, "My students will be way too cool for this." The strategies *were* sometimes unorthodox. "Brain breaks" consisted of one- to two-minute physical or mental challenges that the students tackled every half hour. One brain break involved the whole class standing and writing the alphabet in the air with their index fingers, while counting from one to twenty-six aloud.

The effort to get to Z within one minute helped kids let off steam, and actually increased their focus and positive energy for the rest of the class.

This initially skeptical teacher was amazed when other teachers began praising her students. "What's up with your class?" she heard, "We were in the library today and we couldn't even hear them. How come your students aren't sitting outside the office anymore?" Parents started to report that students had gone home and taught their siblings to calm down through mindful breathing. Something was working. An evaluation report showed that teachers and students found the program effective, behavioural incidents had decreased and students had made some academic gains.

Soon, more affluent schools began to pay attention to what the inner-city schools were achieving. Pedrini tells the story of a teacher working at a very affluent school in Shaughnessy, Canada's wealthiest neighbourhood. Although her students were not burdened with the same hardships as kids in Vancouver's high-poverty public schools, they were under a lot of pressure to succeed and were suffering accordingly. They experienced high levels of anxiety, often let conflicts spin out of control and were extremely self-critical. This teacher's kindergarten-aged son was attending a public school in Surrey, and one day reported that he'd learned to listen at school. He now knew, he said, how to talk to himself "inside [his] head and tell [himself], 'You shouldn't do that, it's not nice.'" The teacher was struck by her child's experience, and began researching Second Step, the program his school was using.

She approached her school's professional development committee with the idea of initiating Second Step, and within a few months, the SEL program had become a school-wide collaborative inquiry project, complete with teacher release time for training. Teachers who had been worried that parents would resent time taken away from academics heard instead that what they were doing was helping their children handle problems, feel successful and build friendships. Social responsibility, with a focus on SEL, has since been made an integral part of the school's mission to develop "creative, independent and mindful graduates."

In a positive bridge between the worlds of research and practice, prospective teachers in B.C. are now required to study SEL. At UBC, Social Emotional Learning is a mandatory course, and all students start their teacher training with a lecture on the subject; they also have the option to join a cohort that will study SEL research and issues throughout their B.Ed., with extra time for in-class experience. Shelley Hymel and her UBC colleagues were also able to obtain philanthropic funding to run a unique graduate course in the field, with a focus on developing the research base around quality programs for schools.

One of Hymel's students launched a field-university working group, called SEL-BC,* that has great influence today. Once a month, twelve districts send one or two people with expertise in SEL to meet, exchange knowledge and solve problems of practice. UBC faculty members share influential research, and the educators talk about what is and is not working in the classroom. The group also sets up partnerships that enable schools to participate in research efforts. Currently, among other topics, SEL-BC is working on developing assessments to help students, parents, teachers and administrators better understand students' SEL needs.

---

* Formerly, the group was called Social Responsibility and Collaborative Learning Environments.

Another of SEL-BC's considerable contributions to the field is a level of quality control. The group helps district leaders select research-backed programs that meet the unique needs of their schools. Because the school system is so decentralized, and there are so many ways of approaching SEL, programs vary wildly and not all are of equal value. Some programs, like SNAP, have detailed processes in place to ensure quality and consistency across schools, including extensive training and support materials and an auditing system. Many SEL programs, however, have never been evaluated, including some that have been widely adopted.

SEL-BC also consults on the customizability of SEL programs at the teacher and school level because, even among evidence-based programs, one size does not fit all. Lianne McBride, the Cindrich teacher who has helped spread self-regulation practices to her school and now to thirty schools across Surrey, has been struck by the importance of program customizability. She has observed that new teachers, or those who are more tentative in their commitment to SEL, appreciate structured programs with clear step-by-step instructions and planned activities, whereas their more confident and experienced colleagues often prefer a less-structured, more inquiry-based approach. McBride believes it is critical that teachers have the freedom to choose among a range of high-quality SEL programs to suit their strengths and their students' specific needs.

The work to get SEL into the classroom is an ongoing process in B.C., but it is gaining momentum. Pedrini estimates that 80 to 90 percent of districts have set goals around the subject, and almost all of them have hired staff leads and resource people in the area. A new curriculum that incorporates SEL practices is now being introduced provincially, and SEL advocates are very enthusiastic about the changes. The new curriculum works SEL expectations into every subject while reducing total curriculum expectations overall. For Pedrini, "the Ministry seems to have learned their lesson about saying 'thou shalt.' Now it's more of an invitation—with some deadlines involved."

There are trade-offs involved in limiting the mandatory aspects of SEL in schools: Not every school has a specific plan around social and personal responsibility, and not every teacher explicitly teaches social-emotional skills. Nor is every school employing a proven program of high quality. But more and more, as awareness of the field and buy-in from researchers, policy-makers and grass-roots supporters increase, programs are spreading and improving.

According to McBride, the new curriculum has made a big difference at Cindrich, clarifying expectations and helping to form a school-wide vision and common language. She believes it has expanded upon the role of teachers and what they can accomplish. "I think there are teachers who believe it's enough that we care about kids," she says. "It's so much more than that. We're all here because we care about kids, but social-emotional learning is about giving the kids the tools to take control of their own learning. I think we still need to grow as educators so we can empower kids, build awareness, and develop strategies."

At the district-level, systems for assessment are being developed. For example, as part of assessing students' ability to identify their emotions, children in grades 3 to 5 might be asked to articulate why characters in a story felt the way they did or how their own emotional state changed at different times during the day. To assess their ability to problem-solve peacefully, they might be asked to generate alternative solutions to a conflict, or explain how resolving a conflict strengthened a friendship.

With its clear policy mandates, support for professional development, strong links between research and schools, and widespread teacher buy-in, British Columbia is a leader at the forefront of SEL innovation at a system-wide level. Having the system behind SEL means reaching all children and not just those whose teachers happen to be interested in the field.

Evidence-based SEL programs are proving their worth, both for students experiencing serious challenges, like Daman, and for those encountering everyday stresses. The Mental Health Commission of Canada is among the most recent organizations to affirm the power, across contexts, of school-wide intervention in the social-emotional skill development of children.[25] Strong social-emotional skills, like self-regulation, growth mindset and peaceful problem-solving, give students the tools to manage themselves and their relationships better, and clear the way for improved learning. They can be taught, and learned, and schools themselves can change to support this learning. Developing these skills is an essential part of preparing students to become leaders who can tackle challenges and persevere, and it sets them up with a foundation for healthy emotional lives.

FOUR

TECHNOLOGY: VOICE, INFLUENCE AND DIGITAL CITIZENSHIP

"If we want students to become smarter than a smartphone, we need to think harder about the pedagogies we are using to teach them. Technology can amplify great teaching but great technology cannot replace poor teaching."
—ANDREAS SCHLEICHER, *Organisation for Economic Co-operation and Development*[1]

Nothing more clearly signals change in schooling than the growing emphasis on information and communication technologies—and the pressing need for students to have the skills required both to engage with this new digital world and to navigate it proficiently. As the digital revolution continues to transform our industries, occupations and even relationships, schools are racing to keep up, with mixed results.

Educational technology spending is burgeoning: according to a *Fortune* article, U.S. venture capital in the field quintupled between 2009 and 2015, reaching two billion dollars.[2] Globally, thirteen billion dollars was invested in 2014.[3] "Digital literacy" is now being touted as a crucial twenty-first-century skill: the ability to access, understand and transform increasingly vast amounts of information; to critique and create a wide variety of media products; and to use technology with skill and ease.[4]

Digital learning is widely seen as the cutting edge of educational reform. And technology does have considerable potential to transform teaching and learning—through flipped classrooms, where lectures are online and class time is used to work on problems as a group; technologically mediated teaching that allows students to go at their own speed or in new directions; or even round-the-world communication and collaboration between peers from different cultures and spaces. Technology has the power to democratize education, making it accessible to the marginalized as never before, and it can provide students with the tools to engender real-world change.

Despite our high hopes and high financial investment, however, most evidence suggests that, so far, technology's impact on schools and on achievement is relatively limited. Are schools hopelessly bureaucratic, ideologically opposed to innovation and staffed by dinosaurs? Are ed tech companies failing to understand, let alone meet, the needs of schools even though they are successfully selling their wares? Or is technology just one tool among many that can facilitate the purposes of schooling, with better and worse ways to deploy it in the classroom?

Opening Up Potential: Innovative Assistive Technology at School

For Corvin Cioata, advances in technology have already been the key to improving his potential for learning—and they are his best hope for a life of relative independence. Corvin was born with cerebral palsy. He experiences significant dystonia, a condition in which muscle spasms significantly limit his control over his movements. Aside from a few words, he cannot speak. Often, his body is locked into awkward and unbalanced positions, so he requires a customized wheelchair.

Nevertheless, his mother, Varinia Vartolas, describes Corvin as a "total communicator. He uses his eyes, mouth, arms. He'll use mime, he goes around a meaning—he'll make you get it." From a very young age, Corvin has had a precocious interest in current events. By age six, he was starting to learn to read from subtitled political debates between Rob Ford and his challengers, or Barack Obama and Mitt Romney. Now a teenager, he tunes in daily to the Weather Network and the local twenty-four-hour news channel, reading the scrolling text and pointing out earthquakes or other out-of-the-ordinary events.

Corvin attended elementary and middle school at Sunny View School, a Toronto public school serving students with multiple and complex disabilities. He, his family, his teachers and a team of specialists worked hard to expand the ways he could communicate. Since he could read, for a time he expressed himself by pointing to the alphabet and to stock messages on an iPad that his mother programmed for him. But the iPad was an imperfect tool: its preset messages were limiting, and Corbin's body restricted his ability to control his gestures, and thus to communicate. His brain would tell his left hand to move, but often it would be his right one that did.

He was fortunate, however, that Sunny View was the home of a school-based initiative called the Infinity Lab. The lab was a partnership between the Toronto District School Board and Holland Bloorview Kids Rehabilitation Hospital, and was substantially funded by a charity started by Sunny View parents. Its goal was nothing less than unlocking communication for a group of children with extremely severe disabilities. New, customized technology—combined with very skilled coaching—allowed ten children a year to actively participate in classrooms for the first time. In its inaugural year, starting in grade 7, Corvin was one of them.

Tom Chau is vice-president of research at Holland Bloorview, and he works to make technology respond to the needs of children with the most serious disabilities. After finishing a doctorate in engineering at Waterloo, Chau went to work at IBM, but, after the birth of his healthy son, decided he wanted to "do something to make an immediate impact on the lives of children and families who were really struggling."

He quit his job, and, as he tells it, stood outside IBM and called up Bloorview MacMillan (as the hospital was then called) to say that he wanted to work with children with major communication issues. He says the hospital thought it was a great idea, but told him not to quit his day job because there was no funding. "It was too late," he said. He felt fortunate to later receive funding for a post-doctoral fellowship, and he's never looked back. There are now between twenty and twenty-five researchers working in his lab, doing remarkable work. Tom has since been recognized as a "transformational Canadian."[5]

With the support of the Sunny View parents' charity, Chau brought his multidisciplinary team to work with a small group of children chosen by the school's teaching staff because the technology had the highest potential to meet their needs. The first step for Corvin, and all the children, was to work with Chau to develop what he calls an "access pathway": anything a child can do independently and repeatedly—move a muscle, make a certain sound—that can be explored as a potential means to operate a communication device. Like many other non-verbal children, Corvin is able to hum through the vibration of his vocal cords, and technology can be used to turn micro-movements like humming into signals. Corvin uses the most common communication device: a neckband, called "the hummer," that contains a tiny sensor that picks up his vocal cord vibrations. The hummer connects through an iPod, and can be hooked up to any communication device—usually, a screen with different images or letters on it.

For some kids, the hummer works like an on-off switch. Those who can control the pitch or length of their hums, like Corvin, have even greater degrees of freedom. Chau has also created similar devices for children who can control their facial muscles or the movements of their tongues. Chau comments, "It's very individual. The basic philosophy is that the child is OK as he or she is, and it's up to us to find the unique ability of each child." Instead of tailoring technology to suit a child's existing abilities, some adaptive technology focuses on training children to manage particular movements or control mechanisms. Learning those movements or controls can take months, and may well result in failure. "Our view is that the onus should be on the technology to accommodate the child."

The next step in the Infinity Lab protocol was "switch training": teaching the children that when they hum, twitch or stick out their tongues, they can create a change in their environment. The students were pulled out of class for switch training, usually with an occupational therapist and an educational assistant (EA). They worked on games to establish the cause-and-effect relationship between their actions and, for example, a balloon bursting on a screen. For some children, this profound lesson—the connection between cause and effect—took some time to grasp because they had previously had such limited ability to exert intentional control over their environment. For Corvin, switch training came relatively easily. Because of his ability to control his humming, Corvin learned to independently activate a switch and operate his communication device, which looks like a regular tablet. He learned to manoeuvre an alphabet screen, linked to word-prediction software, and initiate conversations and share his ideas. With a Bluetooth connection he could work on Word documents on a school computer, or use the large interactive smartboard in the classroom.

Vartolas saw a huge difference in Corvin, noting, "The fact that he has some power in what to choose to say, makes all the difference." She talked about his early years in school, where he often refused to do things, and would sometimes scream out of frustration. His teachers believed he was unhappy, but Vartolas, familiar with his optimism and positive outlook, suspected he actually wanted to learn more, and at a higher level.

With the ability to communicate more of what he wants, Corvin has been able to learn more interesting things, and "his engagement went way up," said Vartolas. For example, by using his device, and working with an itinerant special education teacher, Corvin was able to explore a subject that fascinated him: tornados and their characteristics. He presented his findings to his class at circle time, and even asked other students for their opinions.

A key part of the Infinity Lab process involved training for teachers, EAs, parents and even other students so that the child with special needs could participate fully in their classroom. "Often, even when integrated, children with communication issues will wind up sitting in the back of the classroom with no one talking to them because the other children don't know how to, even if they have the best intentions," explains Chau. Sunny View's special education classrooms were places where everyone worked together to help promote communication.

Chau observed that other students quickly learned to ask yes or no questions, and to wait for answers before rushing on to the next question. Chau laughs at the memory of small children silently counting to eighteen on their fingers in order to allow a classmate enough time to formulate an answer.

Using a range of evaluations, the team found that when teachers, EAs, parents and peers were using the same approach, children made unparalleled gains in communication. It turned out the school was a natural setting in which to help these students achieve their potential and help overcome the loneliness that often accompanies significant communication disabilities. Providing access to other children, and including educators in the training, made a significant difference in children's outcomes.

Vartolas is passionate about her son's potential, and the importance of finding ways to help him access it. She reflected, "If you looked at Corvin, you'd think 'I don't think he can do much.' You have to look into his eyes to see what he can do—this is what is important for him. It's my job to make sure people see him and push him."

After eight years, Corvin graduated from Sunny View and has gone on to Sir William Osler High School, a small school in Scarborough with students who have a much wider range of abilities. He is in a specialized classroom for those with physical disabilities, most of whom can talk. There, with the help of an "incredibly motivating" teacher, as his mother calls her, he's developed new goals, like using his switch device to operate his own electric wheelchair, so he can get around without help. He has been exploring the city on the bus, going on weekly trips with his grandmother to destinations of his choice. He had just come back from the airport when we talked.

Vartolas hopes that with the help of technology and his own learning, Corvin will have more and more opportunities to be independent. She comments, "He doesn't have to be in a normal setting to have a job." They are building on his interest in technology: now, he's messaging friends, filling out online surveys, finding ways to use technology to have his voice heard.

One of the driving forces behind the charity that brought the Infinity Lab to Sunny View was Hayley AvRuskin, mother of two boys at Sunny View, both of whom have severe developmental and physical disabilities. For AvRuskin, setting the Infinity Lab in a school ultimately had considerable ups and downs. On the one hand, being in a school allowed them to build systems around the kids, with many people involved—teachers, educational assistants and students—which amplified the benefits of the initiative. She felt they created a model that others across the province could learn from. Over the past few years, Holland Bloorview has worked with five other schools.

On the other hand, AvRuskin often felt as though she was working uphill in the larger school system. Because of the revolving personnel, parents and advocates were continually re-educating people in the board about the Infinity Lab and its importance. Opaque planning processes—particularly placement decisions that put children with communication issues in a different school—meant that the Infinity Lab initiative didn't last at Sunny View, even while its technology and approach was spreading across Ontario. For its first supporters, the experience with the lab was sometimes as frustrating as it was exhilarating to see children's worlds be "unlocked" by the technology.

Corvin's growing success is just one example of how technology has the potential to transform education, and in some cases even make education possible. At the same time, it underlines the importance of customization based on a deep understanding of students' needs and strengths. Finally, this triumph of technology can only happen in a context where teachers, specialists and families are involved in realizing the potential of the tool.

School in the Cloud

Perhaps the most spectacular claims for the potential of technology come from the world of international development. Because school systems in poor countries are sometimes very weak, the notion that "any change must be an improvement" is pervasive in the Western world, commanding considerable popular press. *The Economist* argued, for example, in favour of the rollout in developing nations of what they called "robo-teaching," where teachers read scripted lessons from hand-held computers that are linked to a central system.[6] Sugata Mitra's TED Talk about a "school in the cloud" has garnered over 2.5 million views.

His "the hole in the wall" computer experiment showed extremely poor children, with little access to formal education, self-organizing to learn complex topics like genetics or, with the help of long-distance volunteers and an Internet connection, English strong enough to work in a call centre. The story is remarkable and compelling—but it also seems to suggest that a computer alone will create revolutionary learning.

The "one laptop per child" project, spearheaded by John Negroponte, former head of the MIT Media Lab, was a larger scale effort to use computers to enable children to "teach themselves" with a super low-cost laptop distributed directly to children. Negroponte, channeling Mitra, told an audience at a technology conference in Lake Tahoe in 2010, "You can give a kid a laptop that's connected and walk away."[7]

The original vision was to distribute 100 to 150 million laptops in the first three years of the program, but growth bottomed out at 1.5 million units after five years. Issues of both implementation and hardware were legion. The computers cost more than anticipated ($188 per unit), and with basic tech support, the estimated cost of $75 per year per student put it out of reach of the world's poorest countries, like Rwanda—which through a donation distributed the laptops to 5 percent of its schools. There, the average annual education budget per student was $109. Other challenges included schools and homes without electricity or Internet, very high breakage rates and very limited use, partially since teachers did not receive training on how to use the technology, or how to teach with it. Most students were using their laptops, if at all, for watching videos.

In a review article on the program, Mark Warschauer of the University of California and Martin Ames of Columbia University concluded that the project had been "naïve and technologically determinist." They argued that proponents of this view tend to see information and communication as tools to be passed out, with simplistic "one-shot" implementation, and that any outcomes are seen to result directly from the technology rather than the work of teachers. Furthermore, these approaches tend to underestimate the challenges of infrastructure and rarely consider whether those on the front line have the knowledge and expertise they need.[8]

The approach of one-laptop-per-child programs in countries like Uruguay, where students' information and communications technologies (ICT) capacity has actually improved, has been the opposite. These programs emphasize the development of appropriate infrastructure and hardware support, and provide in-depth resources for teachers on both the technical and pedagogical aspects of the program.

The ultimate success of technology at school requires careful attention to purpose, context and delivery. The key to digital learning for the vast majority of children will not be a computer by itself, but rather the connection of computer, teacher and purpose—just as we saw with Corvin, who benefited from the *combination* of technology and a school community that supported his learning.

Building in Digital Citizenship, Across the Board

One Montreal school board has launched a large-scale effort to ensure every student is equipped to take advantage of—and remain safe in—the new world of digital learning. Lester B. Pearson School Board, a large suburban English-language school board that runs from the West Island of Montreal to the Ontario border, has established itself as a Canadian leader in the use of educational technology. The board has been intentional and innovative in pursuing the dual goals of ensuring that students have access to educational experiences enriched by technology, and that they are prepared—through an explicit digital citizenship curriculum that runs from kindergarten to graduation—to participate in the Internet in ways that are safe and responsible.

Michael Chechile is the director general of the Lester B. Pearson Board, a position he moved into after spearheading the board's digital citizenship rollout. He shared a series of images with Kelly to explain the goals of the program—showing the World Wide Web as an updated version of the "wild wild west." The board's vision is to take away power from outlaws by putting into place rules and norms that make the Internet a safer and more civil place.

As Chechile remembers it, the transformation at Lester B. Pearson began when he and a group of educators started to "really have issues with technology being blocked." Chief among those issues was the awareness that students will always find a way around the blocks parents or the school system put in place. Blocking access to the unfettered Internet, he argues, is more about maintaining the perception that "everything is under control" than it is about effectively protecting children. Chechile was worried it also sent a message that the Internet was bad. He thought the board needed a different approach, based on the idea that the Internet is, on the whole, good—and the recognition that for students today, there is often a very fine line between the digital and the real world, and that it is therefore critical that they be taught how to navigate both.

Digital citizenship—which gives students a voice and teaches them to take responsibility for their actions online—became the framework for a major policy overhaul. Interestingly, Chechile found support wherever he went. The Council of Commissioners (roughly equivalent to a school board in the rest of Canada) "said go." The Central Student Committee, comprising student representatives from every high school, was completely supportive. Parent consultation sessions were marked by enthusiasm— parents were more interested in their children improving their computer skills than concerned about the potential risks of excessive screen time or unwanted exposure to inappropriate materials. "It was remarkable," comments Chechile. "The more work we did on digital citizenship, the shorter and simpler official policies got."

Notably, student and parent engagement in the digital citizenship program is ongoing. At the beginning of every year, in every class in the board starting in grade 4, students and their teachers negotiate an "acceptable use policy" to establish their rights and responsibilities for technology and the Internet. Students are asked to think through what the rules should be, and these are then formalized into a contract that they bring home to sign alongside their parents. For example, students have access to unlocked browsers, but they have to stay away from materials promoting hate or pornography, and can't share their personal information online. The contract only applies at school, but many parents have adopted it at home, too.

In schools with one-to-one computer programs, where every student buys a laptop, teachers meet with parents to go over the benefits of the program and appropriate uses for the technology. And the board facilitates parent-to-parent digital citizenship training sessions, where parents from each school are trained together; they then go back to their home schools to share what they have learned.

Sometimes, Chechile reflects, the sessions "open parents' eyes to unwanted risks students often experience in their digital lives." Teachers, in particular, keep pushing for students, and their parents, to receive training around digital citizenship at ever younger ages, worried about students posting pictures of themselves on their Instagram accounts in grade 3, and even kindergarten students who described seeing what sounded like porn on home computers. Although the teachers saw it as important to ensure that students and parents were educated about how to respond to the *dangers* of the Internet, Chechile worries there can be too much emphasis on risks, such as cyber-bullying. The digital citizenship program therefore works with students to stress the importance of developing a "positive digital footprint." Chechile believes schools have a role to play in helping students communicate "all the positive things about themselves" in real life and on the web.

Kim Meldrum and Susan Connery are both pedagogical consultants, part of the board's digital citizenship education team who work to help teachers adapt to using new tools in service to their learning goals. For Meldrum, helping students develop a positive digital footprint means harnessing technology to emphasize the broader learning goals of creating, collaborating on and publishing their work from a very early age. She showed me an example: after a field trip to an Algonquian Village, students created animated short films about the daily life of this Indigenous group in the early European contact period. They wrote scripts and created figures and backgrounds to share what they had learned, and they maintained copies of their work in an electronic portfolio.

Pearson has had significant success in getting teachers on board to use technology, mostly through extremely intense and sustained coaching in real-world classroom contexts, which is widely considered best practice in professional development.

Nathalie Charland is an experienced teacher, but when she graduated from teacher's college, technology was not on the agenda at all and, until two years ago, she didn't use it in her personal life. She team-teaches grade 3 with another educator, Anne Jenkins. Charland and Jenkins were asked to start the rollout of one-to-one iPads at Evergreen Elementary School, a beautiful, recently built school in Saint-Lazare, Quebec—a leafy suburb about forty minutes from Montreal.

When she started, Charland described the interactive whiteboard as something that just collected dust in her classroom. An interactive whiteboard allows images to be displayed on a whiteboard using a digital projector. The teacher can manipulate the information by using touch-screen technology. It allows teachers to save notes created in the course of a lesson, transition seamlessly to a site on the Internet and make use of various interactive applications. Many teachers, however, mainly use it as a place to project images. They do not capitalize on the "interactiveness" of the device, reducing it to a very expensive blackboard.

Initially, Charland was quite happy using a blackboard and chalk as her main technology. To push herself to change, she papered over her blackboards—using them to showcase student work, and forcing herself to use the new tools. "You know, you have a bucket list," she explained. "Teaching with technology was on my professional bucket list—but I had a lot of fear. Finally, I said to myself, you've just got to do this." Soon, she was able to use her interactive whiteboard to embed videos into her presentations; invite students to interact with the material on the screen; annotate notes with thoughts from class discussions and save those annotations for later lessons; and use interactive games and activities to keep students focused on the learning at hand.

Her path to becoming a digital educator was eased by something relatively rare in the education field—what she describes as "unending technical support." Susan Connery from the digital citizenship department spent three months working with Charland and Jenkins, helping them plan lessons, access the new tools and programs, and trouble-shoot as everyone used the devices together. They received release time to get to know the tools. Having a teaching partner on the journey made a difference, too. Because they were working with a coach instead of on somebody else's schedule, Connery was able to slow down sometimes, when Charland or Jenkins felt that they were losing the focus on pedagogy.

As anticipated, by starting to work with technology hands-on, they encountered the unexpected and the inappropriate—which, however embarrassing, did create teachable moments. Charland blushes when she remembers the time she ran across the hall to ask Jenkins what the English word for *pivert*, or wood-pecker, is. She returned with the single word written as two ("wood" and "pecker"), and a child earnestly searched the latter, quickly finding a series of inappropriate images. Charland remembers him saying, "Madame, c'est trop gros" before she saw what he'd discovered, and suddenly found herself teaching a lesson about how to respond: tell an adult, turn the screen off. Her response helped teach the children one of the larger lessons of the digital citizenship program.

Now, Charland sees the technology as something that both helps her students be more creative and is "motivating" for them. She describes boys who would normally spend four minutes writing in their journals now using the whole period to write—because of the screen. Many boys thrive when they use visual media, and computers can be an engaging way to improve their literacy skills.[9] Tools like grammar and spell check can be useful as students write, offering them real-time feedback on common errors a teacher would never be able to provide. These self-correction tools allow teachers to devote more time to higher-order thinking skills, like analysis, synthesis and creation—much more important skills in an age when information is so plentiful and readily available. Overall, Charland sees the students in her class take more pride in their work—and put in much more effort—because it looks so good when they are done.

Weak Impact on Teaching or Learning

What Michael Chechile, Kim Meldrum and Susan Connery do *not* say is that students' achievement has improved. In fact, though the board has invested heavily in technology, it doesn't yet have evaluation research about technology's impact on students' performance.

This is typical of the field—it is surprisingly difficult to find independent research on the impact of technology on learning. Of the research that exists, a significant amount is directly funded by technology businesses—or by non-profits and foundations that are indirectly funded by them. Those studies that look beyond abstract tools to classroom practice or impact paint a less than utopian view of the potential of computers. Large-scale studies conducted by governments tend to produce fairly sobering evidence for technology enthusiasts.[10] In the United States, the National Center for Education Statistics (NCES) surveyed 3,159 teachers in a range of school settings to see what sorts of activities students were engaging in online. The 2009 study, based on teachers' self-reports, showed that when teachers used technology, it was most frequently to prepare written text (61 percent), conduct Internet research (66 percent) and practise basic skills (69 percent)—all relatively low-level skills that do not revolutionize classroom learning. Only 25 percent of teachers reported "sometimes or often" using technology to create art or music; 13 percent to design or create products; 25 percent to conduct experiments; and less than 10 percent to have students contribute to a blog or wiki.[11]

At the Pearson Board, too, several teachers Kelly met referenced the usefulness of technology to support basic skills like practice or drill: students, for example, could use apps to learn their dictée vocabulary or, in younger grades, how to form letters. At the same time, however, the Pearson teachers were also using technology in creative ways. Consultants were actively steering teachers toward technological programs that enhance higher-level skills like creativity and reflection: an app to help kids write their own books, for example, or a program that integrates speak-aloud capacity with written and visual tools so that kids can not only solve math problems but easily share their thinking as they tackle them (a well-recognized strategy for improving advanced math skills).

Large-scale, independent evidence casts serious doubt on the impact of technology on *achievement*, which is the litmus test for many system-level decisions about what to emphasize in schooling. In 2015, the OECD released *Students, Computers and Learning*, a report analyzing tests of literacy, numeracy, science, digital reading and computer-assisted mathematics taken by fifteen-year-olds in thirty-one countries or economies around the world. Every participating student also answered a questionnaire that included questions about computer use at home and at school. The OECD team came to a number of conclusions that should provoke reflection on the part of those advocating for enhanced tech investment in schools. Despite the fact that all of the countries surveyed have invested mightily in information and computer technologies over the past decade, there has been no discernable improvement in literacy, mathematics or science test scores over the same period. Moreover, in countries where it is less common for students to use computers at school, students' performance in reading improved more rapidly, on average, than in countries where it is more common. Overall, limited use of computers appears to be better than no use at all, but levels of computer use above the current OECD average is associated with significantly poorer results. The study doesn't find cause and effect, but draws results from large samples across diverse contexts. It raises a range of key questions, particularly: have vital resources been displaced when schools have invested in technology?[12]

Invisible Opportunity Cost

The Lester B. Pearson Board has invested heavily in technology, developed a coherent philosophy behind its use of technology, and put considerable resources into supporting leading-edge digital learning through state-of-the-art, job-embedded professional development. Furthermore, the board has cut costs by asking parents to purchase students' iPads or Chromebooks, and by making extensive use of Google's free software for schools. These decisions have allowed the board to focus its tech budget on superior system-wide wifi improvements and connectivity.

The free Google Apps for Education (GAFE) program provides schools with state-of-the-art software at no cost. The program also comes with online training, detailed privacy protections, ad-free space and the ability for educators to set different types of access for students—for example, children under grade 3 have no Gmail access; and those from grades 3 to 6 have Gmail accounts that only work within the school board. According to Google, this service is provided as a way to "give back" to the educational sector that nurtured the company's early development. Skeptics, however, believe that Google is intentionally creating future markets of users who are most comfortable with Google's tools—a long-term strategy. Similarly, Google claims that it sponsors alluring science fairs to support innovation in school—but the budget comes out of their marketing department.

Even with these creative workarounds to boost technological access for students, the Pearson Board operates in the same environment of tight resources as every school board in the country. Money spent on technology, especially the human resources required to ensure it actually works, has to come from somewhere.

And although classroom time spent on technology *may* increase overall learning time, it often simply replaces other learning activities. These difficult choices about how systems and teachers use their resources illuminate the opportunity cost of technology.

It is hard to trace a direct line from investing in one area to cuts in another—to know exactly what learning opportunities are being displaced. But this year, to balance its budget, the Pearson Board announced that it would no longer employ teacher-librarians in its schools. (After a considerable public outcry, this decision was partially reversed.) The loss of teacher-librarians—and particularly their capacity to promote skills around research, promote choice in reading and carefully select high-quality resources to engage children—would likely have significant educational consequences. Research has shown that the presence of teacher-librarians has a positive impact on students' love of reading, which is one of the strongest predictors of students' overall engagement and academic achievement.[13]

Cash-strapped boards also frequently reduce their investments in textbooks in favour of resources that can be found for free on the web. A study Kelly did for People for Education showed that more than a third of elementary schools in Ontario now most often turn to free online materials when they need new educational resources, due to cuts at the provincial level. Textbooks have many pros and cons, but they can give teachers a starting point so that they can focus more energy on bringing the material alive and less on conducting research. Published materials also generally provide a level of curation and reliability that can be missing from free texts.

Generally, textbooks are subject to some level of oversight for quality and Canadian content. By now, most have taken considerable pains to display, for example, diverse images to represent the whole population, helping students overcome stereotypes and perhaps see themselves in a variety of roles. Kelly visited a grade 4 class at Evergreen School that was using the Internet to complete a project on careers. Not unexpectedly, for unfiltered material, almost every image—scientists, astronauts, writers, mechanics and firefighters—was of a white man. The only women Kelly saw were teachers and nurses. Although educators could, in theory, use the homogeneity of a search engine's images as a teachable moment, some may not take the time to ensure that children see diverse images.

The Citizenship in Digital Citizenship

The *citizenship* in digital citizenship is an important and surprisingly underemphasized aspect of tech learning. At the Lester B. Pearson Board, and really, across North America, the lens of citizenship in the digital realm is pretty strongly focused on individual responsibility. There is an emphasis on ensuring that students understand and develop the capacity to engage with the Internet appropriately and limit harm, and that they are empowered to communicate and create—to "leave a positive digital footprint," explains consultant Susan Connery. There seems to be very little talk about teaching children to use technology to engage with, or even change, the world around them.

There will always be students who are oriented toward activism and a civic sense of responsibility. For example, a group of students across the high schools in the Pearson Board were circulating an online petition when Kelly visited. The petition expressed support for their teachers in a looming strike. The students argued that they shared teachers' interests in reasonable class sizes, supports for students with special education needs, and a well-funded education system where teachers receive good wages and benefits. The students were planning a social media campaign; a letter-writing campaign aimed at the provincial government; and a board-wide student walk-out, with media present, to show solidarity. They also used the petition to ask that the teachers not employ extracurricular activities as a bargaining chip in an upcoming vote, stating, "We are ready and willing to stand by your side, regardless of how your vote goes, but we truly hope that you are willing to stand by ours."

But across North America, there are a few examples of school *systems*—provinces, states or boards—that emphasize specifically the ways in which technology can be used as a tool for citizenship education. Joseph Kahne has done key research in the area of citizenship education, looking at what experiences (in and out of school) help young people become more involved and more thoughtful about life in a democracy. He is the lead researcher on the MacArthur Foundation–funded Youth and Participatory Politics Network (YPPN). The group has begun to focus specifically on the digital dimensions of young people's civic learning opportunities. He explains, "Over the last eight years or so, it has become increasingly clear that if we want to understand young people's political engagement and support it, we need to pay attention to what's going on online."

Students are going online in ways that shape their citizenship—they get information, enter discussions, find ways to mobilize and take action online. In a large representative survey, the YPPN found that more than 40 percent of young people were politically active online, whether that meant being a part of online campaigns, doing research, sharing information about particular issues or creating content—YouTube videos or memes—around political themes. Those who were politically active online were more than twice as likely to get involved in more traditional forms of politics, such as voting or volunteering with political parties. And unlike "traditional politics," in which there is a higher participation of wealthier students with more educated parents, digital participation was equally distributed across different racial and income groups.

As part of its work, the YPPN has connected to real schools and school districts across the United States. One of the most interesting collaborations is with the Oakland Unified School District, a district with a strong investment in changing the status quo. Many of its 90-percent minority, 30-percent English-language-learner families live on very low incomes and in difficult circumstances. In the United States, many school systems have adopted the goal that students will not only graduate, but graduate "career and college ready." In Oakland, the school district has added an additional goal: students will graduate "career, college and *community* ready." A group of about one hundred educators came together to try to decide what that third goal meant, and how to translate it into curriculum. They wanted their students to be able to do issue analysis, have a voice, get involved with others and reflect on their political activities. Some of the curriculum was traditional—debates and simulations, which have been shown over decades to improve kids' engagement in citizenship. But some of it was specifically digital—students were asked to create info-graphics and share them, to do online surveys, and to create blogs and wikis. A number of these Oakland educators formed a group called Educating for Democracy in a Digital Age (EDDA) to support teachers who want to promote citizenship through a mix of digital and traditional forms.

One project the board took on was reforming an existing, district-wide writing assignment for all students in upper-year social studies. To ensure students were graduating "community ready," they gave the project an explicit civic dimension. Last year, students were asked to investigate and take a position on an issue being voted on in San Francisco: raising the minimum wage to fifteen dollars an hour. This issue was seen as particularly pertinent to youth, most of whom work for minimum wage, when they can get work.

Teachers gave kids a variety of materials—online and otherwise. Some teachers sent kids into the community to find out what difference the increase would make for people they knew. Students then turned this research into videos or stories that were shared on a youth-blogging site established with a local community newspaper. Some students conducted polling to gauge public opinion. Polling information was used to make presentations and action plans.

Given widespread concern about low levels of political participation, and particularly, uneven political participation across different groups in society, it makes sense to build upon the digital tools students are already using to promote their civics education.

Linking of student activism with technology has the potential to create real change, as two Toronto teens learned. Their class project on sex education led to a province-wide campaign to ensure students are taught about consent as part of the curriculum. Tessa Hill and Lia Valente were in a grade 8 media studies course at Toronto's City View Alternative School when their teacher, David Stocker, asked the class to work on a year-long independent study project on a social justice issue of their choice. The outcome of their exploration had to be a media product (like a documentary), and it had to include a "call to action."

Stocker emphasized that the purpose of the project was for students not only to learn to use the tools but to gain a sophisticated understanding of the underlying political issue and develop a proactive way to address it. Tessa and Lia credit the course—and the broader school community—for helping them become "learner activists."

Tessa had lived with a dress code, and both girls were interested in how dress codes were enforced. They were interested in "slut shaming" and messages that implicitly or explicitly blame women and girls for the sexual assaults against them by focusing on issues like how they dress. They decided to make a video that looked at rape culture because it was a "part of our lives, media and the everyday lives of so many people." They emphasized that much of their interest arose because they had so much to learn about the subject. Stocker explains, "I always say at the start, 'If you already know everything about your social justice topic, why are you doing it?'" He strongly emphasized the importance of research as an integral part of social justice work—and technology as a key part of the research process.

Students worked together to develop questions and identify experts who could help them learn more. Then, they used email and Skype to contact these leading experts. "Technology allows us to reach people across the planet who spend their entire lives working in the students' fields of interest, and so they are asked to reach for the top," says Stocker.

Through their connection with the experts, Tessa and Lia began to reframe their message from a focus on rape culture to consent culture—the importance of "affirmative, enthusiastic" consent, in the context of sex and more broadly. They were working at an interesting policy moment: Ontario's health curriculum, including sexual education, was in the process of being revised (see also Chapter 7). Both girls were a part of their school's Queer Straight Alliance, and the theme of one of their November meetings was the proposed curriculum revision. Working as a group, the students and their staff sponsor (Stocker again) looked at the limitations of what was being planned. They were shocked to realize that the new curriculum made absolutely no mention of consent to sexual activity, a glaring omission. Suddenly, the girls had a focus for their "call to action." They recognized that although there were many issues of concern around rape culture and consent, the issue of the sex ed curriculum was particularly relevant to them. "Who else should be talking about it but people our age?" said Lia.

One of the goals of the call to action was to support students in taking what they had learned beyond the walls of the school. Once again, digital technology had a key role to play. Tessa and Lia went online in a big way: they created an online petition, started a Twitter account and Facebook page and began sharing the word about their concerns. "Most teenagers know how to use social media already, so it is not such a big step to use it to do activism," Tessa said. In fact, "It's empowering to be able to use something adults are dismissive about—to turn it around and use it for something positive and progressive."

Stocker embraces the use of digital strategies for students' work on social justice—but only when it is accompanied by a thoughtful process. "I see technology as a tool to promote change, but I still think that the underlying political insight and strategy need a lot of focus, so that we aren't left with what's been called 'clicktivism.'"

The power of Tessa and Lia's work came from the intersection of a strong, well-thought-out policy proposal—developed in a collaborative classroom with a focus on citizenship and social justice—and the digital tools they used to connect with experts and to develop and share their ideas. They used their video, Twitter account and an online petition to mobilize others to demand that consent be added to the curriculum. Their message and perspective added a key theme to a broader debate on the sexual education curriculum, and was picked up by traditional media and politicians.

"I cannot imagine having done this without technology," said Lia. Ten years ago, their project might have happened, but it would have been limited to their own school community, perhaps their neighbourhood. "The support we got on social media was a way of meeting the awesome community of activists and feminists. It helped us get our message way beyond our own community." In fact, Tessa says, when word did get out, "online sharing was exponential." The petition went from fifty signatures on day one to one hundred on day two, then to five hundred, one thousand, and thirty thousand a few days later. Soon Lia and Tessa were being interviewed on the radio and in newspapers, and were meeting with the premier. Their campaign was successful: the subject of consent to sexual activity was explicitly integrated into the province's curriculum.

Tessa and Lia acknowledge the support of the entire school community for their social justice project—from their teachers, the principal, other students and even the lunchroom supervisor. Their success is reflective of a school community willing to take risks—specifically, to follow students' lead when they want to talk about potentially charged issues like sex and rape. The school community, particularly David Stocker's class, pushed them to ensure their discussion was well informed, supported their orientation towards activism and helped them engage in that discussion in a very public way.

Stocker doesn't think that students have to be in an alternative school to learn to use digital tools in ways that promote critical, engaged citizenship. But the riskiness of Tessa and Lia's project might explain why active citizenship is not promoted more widely in schools. There are many teachers and administrators who worry about how teaching that engages with controversial issues will affect the comfort level of other students, parents and the broader public. Classes like Stocker's, which explicitly challenge students to look for "upstream" solutions rather than "downstream" ones (for example, exploring causes of poverty vs. hosting a food drive), build critical thinking but also get into the zone where reasonable people disagree passionately. At the same time, Tessa and Lia's powerful stand, risk and all, demonstrates the benefits that can accrue when students are engaged in active citizenship and are supported to speak out about the issues that concern them.

There are places where technology has clearly demonstrated its worth—particularly in special education, whether in the dramatic manner of Corvin and the Sunny View lab, or in the form of more everyday supports for students with different exceptionalities. With the right commitment and genuine personalization built into the learning and social environment of the school, technology can help to advance the goal of making education accessible for everyone. But a healthy skepticism about the benefits relative to the trade-offs is also warranted—and often missing from the discussion. The complexity of budget processes, and the public's enthusiasm for kids having access to technology, sometimes make it hard to assess what is really being gained and what is being lost.

Finally, while we are evaluating technology's impact on pedagogical goals, it is important that our goals extend beyond measureable achievement. The goals of schooling are multiple, and contested, but we are far more likely to create education that contributes to important social outcomes like informed (or even transformative) political participation if we are asking for it. And when technology is reshaping how political participation

takes place in the world outside schools, it creates new challenges and opportunities for schools as places where youth can
shape their own future.

Measuring What Matters

We have already explored several of the ways in which educators
are pushing the limits of traditional education, from building upon
"the basics" and encouraging creativity across the curriculum to
strengthening students' social-emotional skills and promoting acts
of citizenship. These innovations are a win for students and our
society, but from the perspective of the system they are largely
invisible.

Like it or not, the most significant system-level driver for
change in schools today is probably the pressure to boost test
scores. Across rich and middle-income countries internationally,
schools and school systems are judged, and ranked, based on test
performance in a few subjects—most commonly, mathematics,
reading and writing.

It is easy to draw a line between what is measured in large-
scale assessments and resource decisions.[14] In Ontario, for example,
resources have been explicitly funnelled toward improving test
scores. The decision to start province-wide testing in literacy and
numeracy led to the creation of a dedicated agency to oversee the
tests (the Education Quality and Accountability Office, EQAO)
and a Literacy and Numeracy Secretariat within the Ministry of
Education; to the deployment of literacy and numeracy coaches
across the school system; to the implementation of "focused
interventions" for schools receiving low scores; to targeted professional development on literacy and numeracy; and, in most
schools, to the allocation of longer and longer blocks of instructional time for these subjects.[15] More importantly, the government
began to link its main public goals—improving achievement,

reducing gaps and boosting confidence[16]*—to those test scores. As Michael Fullan, then premier Dalton McGuinty's special advisor on education, noted, there has been increasing "congruence" between EQAO test scores and what is happening in classrooms across the province.[17] Measuring matters, therefore, in more ways than one, informing not only what is prioritized in the classroom but what is prioritized in the budget.

Using the resources of a system to promote success, as determined by relatively rigorous consensus goals, sounds like good public policy. Thirty years of international evidence, however, suggests that our current system of measurement, by overemphasizing the importance of test scores, has created real problems.[18] While perhaps not the intention, it has led to the "naming and shaming" of schools, mostly those with highly disadvantaged students.[19] A significant number of educators feel that there is a misalignment between the scores and the most important work that they do in educating their students.[20] Additionally, American evidence shows two disconcerting trends: a rise in rote learning, and the elimination in schools of important subjects that are not tested on international exams, like history.[21]

There may be an even bigger problem built into the design of our current system of evaluation. In the words of Andreas Schleicher, director of the world's most influential testing program, the Programme for International Student Assessment (PISA), "it is obvious that PISA cannot capture the entirety of competencies that will make young people successful."[22] Testing favours primarily the knowledge and skills that we are expert at measuring. Another

---

* For almost a decade, the three system-wide goals for the Ontario education system were: (1) improved levels of student achievement, (2) reduced gaps in student achievement and (3) increased public confidence in publicly funded education. The renewed goals established in 2014 are achieving excellence, ensuring equity, promoting well-being and enhancing public confidence.

major issue identified by Schleicher is that "there is no over-arching agreement on what fundamental competencies fifteen-year-olds should possess." We have designed our system for judging schools' performance—and, in turn, many resource and policy decisions—around a set of subjects and skills that are necessary and yet are not sufficient on their own to prime students and society for success.

Kelly remembers the first time she visited Nancy at George Webster. She was there with Annie Kidder, a fearless public education advocate who was, at the time, her boss at People for Education, and both were blown away by the school. On the walls, they spotted the work of students who were assisting public health officials to assess water quality. In the multi-lingual library, students were working together with energy and co-operation. They met multi-cultural parent ambassadors who were connecting with parents from distinct language communities. In the kitchen, parent volunteers were preparing healthy meals to be shared by all the students. Kelly and Kidder saw signs of a rich, vibrant educational experience all around them, and still this good work had yet to make a dent in the all-important test scores. How could it be, they asked themselves, that we have a system for measuring school success that can't tell that George Webster is a great school?

As an education researcher working on tracking resources in Ontario's public schools, Kelly began to pay more attention to the literature on accountability and testing. While recognizing the disadvantages of large-scale assessment, she also came to understand some of its advantages. It can help prevent kids from slipping through the cracks, identify systemic barriers and provide a measure of tangible, comparable information about the core work of schools. Like most people, Kelly knows how challenging it can be to "get a feel" for a school from a visit only, and can appreciate the appeal of seeing concrete and comparable numerical evidence of progress. Perhaps more than anything, large-scale assessments meet an important communication need between schools, parents and the public.

Kelly began to imagine a more comprehensive set of measures that could communicate a school's strengths across a broader set of educational goals that are equally critical to long-term success, including creativity, citizenship, health and social-emotional skills, alongside literacy and numeracy. And she began to envision an unorthodox way to communicate the importance of these measures to the public and accrue their support.

CBC had just launched *Village on a Diet*, in which a northern British Columbia town with an exceptionally high obesity rate challenged itself to lose weight over fourteen episodes. The show made an effort to highlight strategies at the town and individual level that could help the population to become healthier. Inspired by the program, Kelly began to dream up a competitive reality show to find "the greatest school," in which a group of volunteer schools would compete to demonstrate, for example, the best ways to promote creativity or support active citizenship. The game show format would allow viewers to see concretely what could be happening in schools—and would perhaps encourage the public to start asking schools for goals and action plans around important but too often ignored areas like social-emotional development.

A friend who is a TV producer had to tell Kelly gently that this was not the stuff of television. "You need some kind of narrative arc," she explained. "Schools getting better" is not quite dramatic enough for the small screen.

People for Education, however, took the crux of the idea pretty seriously, despite being actively opposed to school rankings and some of the other problems associated with testing. As an education non-profit with limited resources, a game show was not its terrain, but the People for Education team was interested in finding another way to translate the high-minded goals of inaccessible policy talk into concrete measures that parents could see and feel.

Based on an extensive literature review and conversations with leading experts in government, universities and schoolyards,[23]* People for Education created the project "Measuring What Matters," and landed on a list of five key neglected priorities for schools: creativity, social-emotional skills, health (including mental health), citizenship, and quality learning environments (to measure how well schools' environments were supporting student learning and opportunities). The team believed that these areas were not just critical for schools, but that they could be measured.

From the beginning of the project, People for Education focused intensely on building two-way communication between the general public and educators. In 2013–2014, they hosted face-to-face consultations about their proposed priority areas with over a thousand people, and engaged an additional four thousand in an online survey. Interestingly, 84 percent of respondents believed that the general public "definitely" or "probably" does not understand how schools contribute to students' success in domains like creativity, social-emotional skills, health and citizenship. Nonetheless, People for Education discovered that

---

* Apart from People for Education staff, the team included Dr. Kadriye Ercikan of the University of British Columbia (national leader in educational assessment); Dr. Charles Ungerleider, emeritus professor of education and a former deputy minister in British Columbia, Dr. Rena Upitis of Queen's University (creativity); Dr. Stuart Shanker, then of York University, now of the MEHRIT Centre (social-emotional skills); Dr. Bruce Ferguson of SickKids Hospital's Community Health Systems Resource Group (health); and Dr. Nina Bascia of the Ontario Institute for Studies in Education of the University of Toronto (quality learning environments).

there was very strong support for their proposal: 88 percent of those surveyed supported the idea of setting goals around health, creativity, social-emotional skills, citizenship and quality learning environments, and 78 percent supported measurement of these areas.

People for Education is not looking for schools to "do more with the same resources," but rather to distribute their resources more proportionately across a range of valuable competencies. For Kidder, "in putting pressure on schools and the government to change what they report on and the things they know how to measure, we might change public feeling about the role and purpose of public education." In essence, the hope is that it might create a greater sense of public responsibility for the schools of the future.

Perhaps the most ambitious project in People for Education's history, the guidelines of Measuring What Matters and the new lexicon built around them are now seen as an innovative model of best practice across several international networks—for example, the Brookings Institute asked People for Education to be a partner in their global Learning Metrics Task Force. The team has also garnered a formidable group of supporters and funders who have helped to feed the project. Kidder and People for Education research director David Cameron have brought the project, now in its third year, to twenty-six schools across Ontario, and are working with them to translate the five domains into measureable competencies. The sheer number of competencies can be daunting: there are ninety-six. In the domain of creativity, Measuring What Matters defines five separate competencies, including whether students are imaginative. Under each competency is a list of "look-fors." If students are imaginative, they will make connections across disciplines and between objects and ideas. Imaginative students will use intuition and apply metaphorical thinking. At this point, before it makes sense to develop specific measurements, the project is focused on reaching an agreement on workable definitions and priorities for each domain. For now, different educators "measure" these competencies in different ways. Some use notes from observations of students; others use student work samples; others use student self-assessments and others document conversations between students and teachers, or students and their peers.[24]

While it is not a straightforward process, People for Education sees Measuring What Matters as an important way to help the education community adopt a means of assessing and communicating the skills and competencies that experts, business and civic leaders have identified as so important. By putting pressure on the government to change what it reports on—and, therefore, what it takes responsibility for—the hope is to help change public feeling about the role and purpose of public education.

"Public education has a role to play in the health and strength of the country," says Kidder, "we are literally building the next generation of society. In Canada, 95 percent of children attend public schools. They are essential for individuals, our communities and our country. We are preparing young people to live healthy, economically secure, civically engaged lives where they can innovate and solve complex problems."

Measuring what matters in schools may be complex, but it is vital—and possible.

FIVE

SCHOOLS OF CHOICE

"The most fundamental choice of parents in a public school system is the right to enrol their children in a school where they can learn with their peers. School choice is not a right when it has a negative effect on the educational provision of other children, especially those who are most vulnerable."

—J. DOUGLAS WILLMS,
The Case for Universal French Instruction[1]

B ogdan Knezevic, Canadian Rhodes Scholar and member of the Serbian Olympic swim team, immigrated to Southern Ontario when he was three and a half years old. A bright and active little boy, he started junior kindergarten speaking only Serbian. When his teacher remarked upon his poor language skills, his mother was prompted to ask her why, then, she wasn't *teaching* him English. This teacher had low expectations for Bogdan, and she did not understand how to push him—or how transformative pushing him could be.

After that rocky start, Bogdan began to thrive. His grade 1 teacher was impressed by his creative abilities, and would send him to the principal's office to read his stories to the secretaries. His grade 4 teacher recommended that he be tested for gifted verbal and spatial ability, and Bogdan was "screened in" to the Enhanced Learning Program in the Peel District School Board.

In the Enhanced Learning Program, Bogdan noticed an immediate difference in the kinds of work students were asked to do—projects and presentations that explored wide-ranging, real-world subjects, which "helped prepare [him] for what [he] had to do later on." Students were encouraged to explore their interests and to aim high. If children were struggling, Bogdan thought teachers were more likely to work with them than educators in regular programs—perhaps because the students had already demonstrated their potential or because these teachers were better equipped to guide their students through challenges. When his family moved neighbourhoods, Bogdan insisted upon remaining in the program. His father would drive him back and forth every day so that he could attend school without missing his 6 a.m. and 4 p.m. swim practices around the corner from their home. Bogdan believes that this specialized program started him down his path of academic and athletic success.

In the last decade, there has been a boom in specialized programs in Canada's elementary, middle and high schools: enriched "mini schools;" alternative, gifted and Aboriginal-centric programs; sports academies; French and Mandarin Immersion; International Baccalaureates; and more. The Vancouver School Board's eighteen secondary schools boast no fewer than fifty-two specialized programs, Calgary is home to six charter schools and over fifty alternative programs, and half of the Toronto District School Board (TDSB)'s secondary schools identify as specialty schools of one kind or another. In the TDSB, the percentage of students enrolled in specialized programs (30 percent total) doubled between 2003 and 2013, and in gifted programs, enrolment tripled.[2] As one downtown principal commented, "There are so many schools in this neighbourhood, you don't have the option of just being a community school."

These so-called schools of choice are on the rise because many parents believe they provide an elevated educational experience. The vast majority of Canadian Rhodes Scholars over the last several years have been public school graduates, and more than half have attended specialty programs. Like Bogdan, most of the scholars we interviewed for this book consider those programs to have been central to their success. For Brittany Graham, the opportunity to pursue her early passion for writing through a specialized arts education led to "the best high school experience anyone could ever have." When asked what had made her school experience outstanding, she reflected,

> I got great feedback, one-on-one relationships, teachers who paid attention to me. I had these teachers telling me to keep going, your work matters. That's a really strong message to have from someone who is not a parent. It is important that students get to do something they really love. . . . Everybody was loving school because of art, and that love spilled over into all the classes.

Brittany's writing flourished, as did her interest in her other courses. She was ultimately inspired by her grade 11 biology course to pursue a career in the sciences—to great success.

Research does show that when students have the opportunity to choose their school, they are more likely to feel connected to its community and vision, which in turn positively affects motivation, engagement and performance.[3] And often, students who are already thriving do even better when they encounter higher expectations, a more challenging curriculum and a stronger peer group. A 2010 TDSB report on French Immersion, alternative schools, International Baccalaureate, and specialized arts and sports programs found that, overall, students in these programs demonstrate above-average achievement.

Evidence also suggests, however, that schools of choice exacerbate patterns of social stratification along lines of income, race, parental education and disability. The TDSB report found that, overall, students who attend alternative and specialized schools and programs are more likely to come from families that have parents with higher levels of education and a higher social economic status, and a two-parent family structure.[4] Schools and programs of choice have fewer students with special education needs and fewer minority and immigrant students: 91 percent of French Immersion students in grades 9 to 12 were born in Canada, versus 64 percent of students in the wider TDSB; 62 percent of French Immersion students in these same grades identified themselves as white, versus 29 percent across the school board.

By and large, it is students who are already privileged in some way who are reaping the rewards of specialized education. And despite the variety of ways in which one can access specialty programs—applications, lotteries, auditions and portfolios, entrance exams or psycho-educational screening using standardized measures like IQ tests (often based on teacher recommendations or parent funding)—their socio-economic makeup is not changing.

Since her extraordinary high school experience, Brittany has had to confront the inequality of the education system. Her boyfriend of five years, Jarrett, is from the Saugeen Ojibwe First Nation, a community of 150 people on the shores of Lake Huron near the Bruce Peninsula. The closest public school is twenty kilometres away, in Owen Sound. There, no specialized programs were on offer, but students were meant to have a choice between academic and applied streams in math, English, science, geography, history and French. Jarrett and all of the children from the reserve, however, were automatically enrolled in the applied courses. As discussed in earlier chapters, although academic and applied streams are supposed to be equivalent, research makes clear that students in applied courses suffer comparatively. Whatever their prior level of achievement, they perform less well on provincial tests[5] and are less likely to move on to post-secondary education.

Brittany reflected, "It was really shocking for me, because I had had so many opportunities. Not only did Jarrett and his friends not get the encouragement that I got, teachers and guidance counsellors assumed that they were not capable of doing great things simply because of their home community." When she went on to work in the Eabametoong First Nation in Fort Hope, Ontario, she realized that students' "choices" are often even starker than she had imagined. "I wouldn't have finished high school if I had had to leave my family and live with a foster family, or had to attend a school where I had experienced racism."

How can parents choose the best school for their children without reinforcing inequity? And how can schools of the future address, and reduce, the performance gap between specialized programs and all the rest?

Difficult Choices
We have had to ask ourselves these questions.

Kelly's children are in a French Immersion program. She was thrilled that, through the Canadian public education system, her kids could receive deep exposure to another language. And they have done pretty well in school so far. Over the years, however, Kelly has seen first-hand that the program does not serve all children equally. Increasingly, she has seen her children's friends with special education needs leave the program. Some of their parents worried the educational supports in the program were too weak, others decided their children did not need to struggle to learn French in addition to their other challenges. She has also witnessed the French Immersion program affect the diversity of the school's population. One of the ways in which the TDSB has tried to address the growing demand for French immersion is by limiting the catchment area for schools. This "zoning" decision has made her children's school visibly less diverse than it was when her son entered kindergarten eight years ago.

Kelly and her family felt the sting of "losing the lottery" for her son's middle school. The small program she had hoped he would attend emphasizes real-world application and social justice—with units on designing your own town, learning about the world through the United Nations and performing a mock trial for Louis Riel. The teachers consciously experiment—at the time, they were running a two-year pilot on the impact of late starts to the school day. And having observed gendered patterns of participation in science class—where girls were reading instructions and doing the write-ups and boys were conducting the hands-on running of experiments—they tried to disrupt the patterns by teaching science separately to boys and girls, giving each a fuller range of educational experiences. For the 2015–2016 school year, 250 applications were received, from across the whole city, for only thirty-six spots. And unfortunately, there is no other program like this one in Kelly's neighbourhood. Kelly knows her children are fortunate, and feels lucky that most of the schools in her community are pretty good. Her son, in fact, thrived at the school where he wound up. Like all parents, however, she wants more than "pretty good" for her kids—but she doesn't quite know how to reach it, and to some extent, having the choice slightly out of reach made her feel worse about what was available.

Nancy had a similar dilemma when, in grade 3, her son began to disengage from his studies. Although his school had a good reputation, Nancy could see that her son was not being pushed far enough. This had been an issue since he was in grade 1: during parent-teacher interviews, his teacher had reported that he could count to twenty, which was the expectation that needed to be met in that grade. But Nancy knew that her son could count by 11s to 121. The teacher was making sure her son could meet the requirements, and had no idea that he could do so much more. For Nancy, that typified too many mainstream classrooms, where students are often unintentionally limited by their teacher's well-meaning but unspectacular expectations.

Nancy ended up enrolling her son in a gifted program, but with some ambivalence. The subject of her master's thesis had been gifted education, and she had concluded that all students should—and *could*—have access to the methods recommended for gifted students. When all teachers are supported and expected to focus on big ideas and higher-order thinking as much as skill and drill activities, gifted classes become unnecessary. As the staff at George Webster demonstrated with their school-wide, problem-solving initiatives (like the Radical Math project described in Chapter 1), this is possible. This type of learning, however, was not happening in the regular classrooms at her son's public school.

When Nancy's son entered the gifted program, his motivation and performance initially improved. He responded to his teacher's expectations for him, working harder than he ever had before to meet them. The next year, however, the limits of gifted education became clear. Her son's new teacher had no expertise in enriched education; when Nancy asked her what practices she would be employing to specifically engage gifted students, she had no answer. All teachers require a repertoire of skills to meet the needs of the children in front of them, and this teacher did not seem particularly invested in improving. Almost any teacher can be good enough when willing to learn what is needed. There is no reason a teacher in a gifted program should not be using "gifted" strategies.

A Specialty Program Done Right

Monarch Park Collegiate is located in a neighbourhood on the east side of Toronto that has been characterized by high levels of immigration and relatively low incomes.* In 2006, the school was experiencing a low point. The Fraser Institute had ranked it among Ontario's bottom ten schools due to low math and literacy scores. And of an overall population of about a thousand students, only thirty-five kids had enrolled in grade 9.

By 2012 and 2013, Monarch Park was named the fastest-improving school in the province by the same organization, with test scores solidly in the middle of the provincial range. Principal Rob MacKinnon, one of Canada's Outstanding Principals, led the process of transformation in his first year at the school. The first step was to tackle a pair of linked challenges: developing and giving substance to a coherent vision for the school and improving its reputation in the community. Inspired by the seventy-five languages already spoken between the students and staff, MacKinnon and his team worked together to build up Monarch Park's identity as a global school. They incorporated global themes into every course, and forged a partnership with Canadian charity Free the Children, which provided students with many exciting, real-world learning opportunities. For example, a course was developed in which students travelled to Kenya to conduct development work while studying the broader socio-political contexts involved.

Beyond these school-wide changes, Monarch Park applied for International Baccalaureate (IB) certification. The mission of this internationally certified, highly structured and academic program is to "develop inquiring, knowledgeable and caring young

---

* The school came to public attention in the summer of 2016 when Canadian swimming phenom and Olympic gold medallist Penny Oleksiak was identified as a student at the school.

people who help create a better and more peaceful world through intercultural understanding and respect." The program's best practices are actually quite similar to those found in public schools across Canada—high expectations, active learning, developing social skills alongside academic learning, a strong focus on critical thinking and skilled research—but it has strong measures in place to ensure these are realized. The program is subject to external monitoring through test-score reporting and bi-annual program reviews. And of course, the particular students admitted to the program facilitate the program's success. John Au, a science teacher who became the coordinator of Monarch Park's IB program, noted: "By definition, an IB program, being a magnet program, brings engaged children and parents into the fold—they have to apply, there is an interview."

At the time, there were three IB programs in the TDSB (there are now eight). Monarch Park was able to make the case to the board that it needed the boost an IB program would provide to help it thrive: it made sense, from an equity perspective, to put an IB program in a school with many socio-economic challenges. As Principal Rob MacKinnon argued, "Why shouldn't these kids, in this community, have the same access to programming that was available in neighbourhoods with wealthier populations?" Unlike many specialized and alternative programs, in order to increase accessibility for all, students with special education needs were included in the IB program and received the necessary accommodations and support.

The IB program immediately attracted positive attention to the school. Au remembers only one family attending the school's open house the year before it received IB certification. The following year, there were 160 families present, and later more than 500. The IB program gave the school the academic legitimacy it was lacking, and boosted its overall reputation.

MacKinnon stresses, however, that it was key to the school's new vision that students in *all* programs "be part of a fantastic community moving forward together," without any one group being perceived as elite. The school made a decision not to house different programs in different wings, so that all students would have the opportunity to mingle. And at the beginning of grade 9, all of the students—across the IB, special education and regular programs—went on a camp field trip together. It was difficult to find a camp that could accommodate students with significant physical disabilities, but ensuring that every student could attend was a priority, in order to build the cohesion that the school was seeking. And, perhaps most importantly, and unusually, Monarch Park's teachers worked across all programs. Every teacher in the school was familiar with "gifted" methods, and could apply those in any classroom. Teaching strategies and priorities from the IB program began to permeate the larger school, such as an emphasis on critical thinking, collaboration and empathy. And as Au notes, this method boosted teacher engagement, too—it was "more interesting for the teachers, and made better use of their skills."

Jacqui Strachan is a former lawyer and a long-time education activist. When she visited Monarch Park to consider it for her son, she wasn't interested in its IB program. Overall, academics were not her primary concern. It was most important to Strachan that her son, who was not always motivated in the classroom, feel included and valued at school. She chose Monarch Park for its "incredibly warm" environment and staff, and for the school-wide emphasis placed on rich, real-world education. After her son enrolled, Strachan joined the school council and was its chair for several years. She described the school's "relentless" efforts to develop activities that met the needs of the whole student population.

Monarch Park is a great success story and one model for schools of the future. Academic magnet programs can positively affect a school's overall reputation and drive enrolment. And when their resources are shared school-wide, and every student is made to feel connected to the institution's vision and community, specialized programs and strategies can benefit every child in the building.

System Perspectives

The inequity perpetuated by schools of choice poses a significant challenge on a systems level. New Brunswick is an example of a province that has tried to respond to this problem—with mixed results. In 2008, the provincial government tried to abolish its Early French Immersion program after two government-appointed commissioners issued a damning report on its efficacy and outcomes.[6] At that time, New Brunswick, the only officially bilingual province in Canada, had the largest French immersion program in the country, with over 20 percent of non-francophone students enrolled. Commissioners Jim Croll and Patricia Lee found that only 37 percent of students who attended Early French Immersion stuck with the program through to grade 12. And of those who persisted long enough to be assessed, fewer than half achieved an "advanced" level of proficiency.

The commissioners also cited "the negative impact on the system caused by the streaming of students." They found that many parents placed their children in the immersion program to give them a "'private school' experience in a public school setting" and to keep them removed from children with discipline issues and special education needs. Superintendents interviewed for the report said that parents saw the core English programs as "ghetto schools." Croll and Lee went on to conduct a statistical analysis that showed that the percentage of children with exceptionalities in French Immersion was 4.6 percent, compared to 23.6 percent in the English stream.

They recommended that Early French Immersion be eliminated in favour of intensive French language instruction for all students starting in grade 5, with a late immersion program beginning in grade 6. They advised that French Immersion teachers receive special education training, and that students of all abilities be encouraged to apply to the specialized program.

Shortly thereafter, Professor J. Douglas Willms, a Canada Research Chair at the University of New Brunswick who has had an enormous impact on the study of Canadian children as the lead investigator for the National Longitudinal Study of Children and Youth, released a supporting report. Willms used postal code data to analyze French Immersion enrolment in New Brunswick by socio-economic status (based on family income, education and occupation). Dividing the population into five groups, he found that those from the most affluent and best-educated group were more than twice as likely to enrol their children in French Immersion than the middle group. In turn, those in the middle group were twice as likely to enrol as those from the lowest groups. Forty-two percent of those in French Immersion were from the highest socio-economic status group, and only 12 percent from the lowest. Like Croll and Lee, he also concluded that there were far more students with special education needs and behavioural problems in core English. Willms insisted the current program was *harming* students in the English stream, calling the process "segregation." These patterns of inequality, he argued, were depressing overall achievement outcomes for the province, which were below the Canadian average.[7]

Just two weeks after the release of both the Croll and Lee and Willms reports, the minister of education released two regulations eliminating Early French Immersion, effective the following fall. To say that this decision caused an uproar is an understatement. It led to vociferous—and ultimately successful—public campaigns,[8] from protests (including Acadian-style, pot-banging Tintamarre, videos of which went viral), petitions, letter-writing campaigns, weekly sit-ins at the MPP's office, alliances with national groups like Canadian Parents for French, and more.

The French Immersion parents made a number of arguments. Their most powerful, perhaps, was that the minister's new policy would impose mediocrity on students by forcing a less-effective model of immersion upon them. They pointed to statistics to show that early immersion, which begins in grade 1 in New Brunswick, is better for the mastery of French than late immersion, which begins in grade 6. They argued that it would be better to invest in proper supports to ensure all children had access to Early French Immersion, and to do more to promote the advantages of bilingualism across all classes. They faulted the current system for failing to provide support to students who were struggling in French, thus exacerbating the differences between the programs. The early immersion program was particularly important, in their view, because it could give children who did not have social class advantages access to language learning—a potential golden ticket.

Within three months, the dissenting parents created a group called Citizens for Educational Choice and took the case to court. They argued that the minister's decision violated their rights, breached a contract and represented a failure of natural justice. Justice Hugh McLellan of the Court of Queen's Bench, in a ruling issued in June 2008, did not come to a conclusion on their rights or contract, but agreed that the process for consultation had been "unfair and unreasonable" and that parents who had enrolled their children in the program for the fall "had a reasonable and legitimate expectation that program would not be cut without them having a real opportunity to be heard by the minister."[9]

In consequence, the momentum behind the policy change came to an abrupt halt. Within two weeks, the minister proposed an amended approach that restored Early French Immersion starting in grade 2, maintained late immersion starting in grade 6, moved the oral proficiency test from grade 10 to grade 12 and required all students to learn together in their final two years of high school. After a six-week online consultation, the new plan was adopted. The issue continued to plague provincial governments—the Liberals ran the province from 2006 to 2010, and the Conservatives from 2010 to 2014. The Liberals returned to power with a promise to reinstate Early French Immersion: grade 1 entry is scheduled to resume in September 2017, with many school boards expressing concern about whether they would have qualified teachers in place to deliver the program.[10]

The case of New Brunswick can be read several ways: it is at once an exceptional story of parent engagement and activism and an example of the political power and privilege of those at the top of the socio-economic chain. And it implies that a frontal attack on the stratifying impact of programs of choice will face serious resistance.

How then can this imbalance be mitigated on a systems level? One strategy is to improve the supports available in specialized programs, to reduce their exclusivity and make them more accessible to students with special education needs. There is a pervasive fear among parents that academic programs will be diluted if they include children with special needs. But as many of the schools featured in this book reveal, abilities are not static and good teaching in any setting can be transformative.

Parents and teachers will need to keep working to dismantle stereotypes about who is, and can be, a good learner.

Another strategy is to spread enriched practices more broadly—using projects, field trips and real-world experiences to root learning and encourage critical thinking, and projecting high expectations onto all children. At Monarch Park, there was a real effort to ensure that the same educators teaching IB were also teaching special education and applied courses, so best practices could be spread easily throughout the school.

Gifted students should not need a gifted program to thrive, and children should not need to seek out alternative programming to receive real-world, authentic, engaging and topical learning. Indeed, the kind of inquiry-based, enriched learning practices found in gifted programs is the same kind recommended for teaching critical twenty-first-century skills. Those skills that were once considered necessary for only the brightest students are skills that everyone in this rapidly changing age of information now needs in order to thrive.

SIX

SCHOOLS CAN'T
DO IT ALONE

"Some critics urge that educators should not acknowledge socioeconomic disadvantage because their unique responsibility is to improve classroom practices, which they can control. According to such reasoning, we should leave to health, housing and labor experts the challenge of worrying about inequalities in their respective fields. Yet we are all citizens of this democracy, and educators have a special and unique insight into the damage that deprivation does to children's learning potential."
—RICHARD ROTHSTEIN, *"Whose Problem Is Poverty?"*[1]

It was through her father's work that Nancy became aware of the idea that schools could, and should, do more than just teach the 3Rs. Dr. Paul Steinhauer was one of Canada's leading child psychiatrists and the first director of training at the world-renowned Hospital for Sick Children (now SickKids) in Toronto. He understood that children thrive through the collaboration of the larger systems that envelop them. He believed that there are three keys to unlocking better outcomes for children. First, he thought it was critical that society focus on catching problems early, at their root causes, to prevent more serious harm later in life. He likened the approach of treating mental health only in adulthood to a man standing by a river and watching a torrent of dead bodies float by. The man is busy pulling bodies out of the river, but surely it would make more sense to go upstream to halt the source of the crisis. Nancy grew up hearing her father proclaim that one dollar spent early in a child's life would save seven dollars later on.

Second, he believed that the best way to resolve challenges facing young people is for interdisciplinary teams to work together. To illustrate this point, he would tell a story of six blindfolded men and an elephant. Each man could feel a different part of the elephant's body, and came to a different conclusion about what was before him; it was only when the six men combined their findings that they were able to figure out what they had encountered. He had been involved in situations in which actual harm had occurred because families had consulted different specialists whose solutions worked against one another.

Finally, his experiences as a child psychiatrist attuned him to the critical role that families play in children's overall well-being, and the difference it can make when schools work closely with them. When families and schools are consistent in their messaging and expectations, children are more likely to overcome challenges. Conversely, when families feel excluded from decisions made by schools, it can hinder children's progress. Schools that engage parents and offer supports to the whole family can in turn boost their students' ability to learn.

Bringing Families In

The Toronto District School Board (TDSB) collects information about parents' attitudes toward schooling at every level of income. Between the highest and lowest income groups, there are negligible differences in the interest parents demonstrate in the home: how often they speak to their children about school and help them set goals and make plans. Beyond the home, however, involvement differs. Research shows that parents' direct participation in schools varies considerably depending on their income and education; families facing poverty and other socio-economic challenges are much less likely to be active in the day-to-day workings of schools.

Nancy witnessed this discrepancy first-hand. Her first teaching job was at an elite independent school. Her classroom was right by the school's front door, and every day at 3:15, she could expect a crowd of parents to peer through the classroom window, examining her every move. The parents scrutinized the school, and felt empowered to question its workings and challenge the teachers' decision making. Nancy enjoyed these conversations. They taught her how to articulate the thinking behind her actions and evidence behind her practices, and to collaborate effectively with parents. In 2006, she became the principal of a small public school in Toronto's much-maligned Jane and Finch neighbour-hood. A 2010 survey of the area revealed that residents are from eighty ethno-cultural groups and speak over 112 languages. Households were far more likely to have children under nine-teen and far more likely than average to be led by a single parent; almost 30 percent of adult residents had not finished high school and as many were living below the low income cut-offs estab-lished by Statistics Canada.[2] Tensions were particularly high when Nancy started, after a headline-making summer of unprec-edented gun violence.

Nancy didn't know the area well, and was keen to meet the staff, students, parents and larger community. She and the out-going principal decided to organize a meet-and-greet breakfast event so Nancy could connect with parents and caregivers. The day before the event, the teacher-librarian, an established mem-ber of the community who had been at the school on and off since the year of Nancy's birth, distributed flyers to parents adver-tising the breakfast.

Not one parent showed up. Nancy, the teacher-librarian and the outgoing principal were alone in the library with hun-dreds of muffins and more coffee than they could drink. At one point, the current principal dragged the school council chair over from the kitchen, where she had been preparing a snack for the students. The chair greeted Nancy, and then shyly asked if she could continue preparing the snack. Alongside one other mother, she made snacks daily for over four hundred students, and she had a deadline to meet.

It would be a challenge to get to know the parents and care-givers of the students, and to ensure that they had a strong voice in the running of the school. The extreme poverty faced by many of the parents and the weak social networks surrounding them appeared to generate mistrust—and this, in turn, had a distinct impact on students' readiness to learn. That first year, the staff spent considerable energy thinking up creative ways to get parents out to school council meetings. They combined the first meeting and a community barbeque with curriculum night, to take advantage of parents already being in the building. Their strategy worked, with almost thirty parents ultimately attending the event. The school then used a survey to identify areas of concern for parents—how to raise good readers, how to manage stress—and brought in staff from the library, Toronto Public Health and other outside organizations to ensure meetings were as useful as possible. Nancy and her vice-principal learned how to be more flexible, often arranging to be at the school on weekends and evenings so agencies could offer services without incurring permit fees required by the board. Slowly, the parents became a larger part of school life. By the time Nancy left to go to George Webster, two years later, there were healthy numbers at school council meetings, one indicator that parents' feeling of belonging in the school was improving.

One experience early in her tenure at George Webster revealed to Nancy the distance between the school and members of the community, as well as the vital importance school, as a place of engagement and safety, might play in the lives of students. Soon after Nancy started at George Webster, she encountered Christina. A petite nine-year-old with long black hair, big blue eyes and an angry mouth, Christina was a capable student, but she easily leapt into defiance with her teachers, and seemed to derive some pleasure from making other students miserable. She spread rumours about other girls and provoked fights with boys. Constant adult supervision was required to stem her cruelty. Conversely, she was adept at working with younger students and enjoyed helping out in the kindergarten room.

One day, well after the school bell had rung, a young Tamil-Canadian boy came to the office crying. He had been riding his scooter in the yard when Christina forced him off it and rode away, leaving him stranded. Nancy reassured the boy and his mother that she would get his scooter back. Since one of her goals for Christina was to keep her out of trouble with the law, Nancy chose not to get the police involved. First, she tried to contact Christina's mom, but she was hard to reach. The cellphone on record changed frequently, and even when the number was working, Christina's mother would rarely pick up or return calls. She would on occasion call the school to protest a punishment that had been imposed on Christina, insisting that her daughter had been unjustly accused; other times, she would publicly berate Christina for the problems when confronted. It was difficult to predict how she'd respond—and whether she would respond at all.

Christina's mother was young, with a toddler, so Nancy thought her best chance of making a meaningful connection with Christina and her mother was to visit them at home. They lived in one of the large apartment buildings about two blocks away from the school. The next day at lunchtime, Nancy called Christina down to the office. Christina didn't exactly acknowledge to Nancy that she had stolen the scooter. But when Nancy asked Christina to take her and another teacher to her apartment so that they could retrieve and return the scooter, she acquiesced. Leading them through the backyard of the school and down the street to the entrance to her building's parking lot, Christina manoeuvred her way through the tunnel of cars toward another unlocked door into a poorly lit hallway in her building.

The one working elevator was crowded and tense. No one spoke. On the ninth floor, Nancy knocked on Christina's door. At first, no one answered. Harder knocking prompted yelling from the other side. Christina's mother opened the door a crack and quickly ushered Christina into the apartment, slamming the door. Nancy and the teacher waited for Christina to reappear with the scooter, which she did, her mother nowhere in sight.

The elevator took its time. When it arrived, it took the group and the scooter up to the fourteenth floor, then back to the ninth, back up to the fourteenth floor, and back down to the ninth. The elevator went through this ritual one more time before continuing down to the ground floor, with many stops along the way. Suddenly, it was clear to Nancy why many of the students living in this building were habitually late.

The visit to Christina's taught Nancy something about the reality of some of her students' lives. Many of the students' families were just getting by—unemployed or underemployed, struggling to make ends meet. Their living conditions were often unpleasant and even unsafe. For many of the students, George Webster was a home away from home—cleaner, more spacious and more tranquil than where they lived. Part of the challenge was to ensure that students knew that they, and their families, really belonged there, and to make sure the space was open and useful not just to students but to their parents.

One of the ways schools can build kids up is by building up the whole family, giving parents the tools and services they need to be better caregivers and encouraging them to be advocates for their children's education.

———

One of the most exciting aspects of the Model Schools for Inner Cities approach was the innovative Parent Academy program Nancy experienced during her time at George Webster. Through the Parent Academies, clusters of schools pooled their resources to provide parents with opportunities for professional and personal growth. Created for and by parents, these educational events were designed with the goal of increasing parent voice and leadership. Sometimes, this meant practical courses like first aid and food handler certifications to boost parents' chances of employment, a critical issue with a big impact on family stress— and ultimately, on children's achievement. Some of the grads from the food handler course went on to find part-time work, including some as lunchtime supervisors at their children's schools. Other workshops tackled broad social issues like gender equality.

When Ingrid Palmer walked through the door of the principal's office on a hot June day, the school was not the same place it had been a few years before. Through the dedication of the school's staff, George Webster had been transformed into a vibrant community hub. Palmer was nonetheless concerned. She was considering sending her son to George Webster, and word on the street was that it was still a fairly rough place.

George Webster had offered Palmer's son a placement in a diagnostic kindergarten class, designed for students who are unable to cope in a larger setting. The class would have only eight students, a teacher and an educational assistant, as well as access to an occupational therapist and a speech-language pathologist. The placement sounded ideal, but Palmer wanted to be certain that the school would truly meet her child's needs. Her son was a quiet boy, high-functioning with autism, and school could be challenging for him. He didn't know how to connect with other children, and he wasn't toilet trained. In junior kindergarten, Palmer had had to go to his school four times a day to change his underwear and clothes.

School had always been an important part of Palmer's life, but she had had a range of experiences with it—not all positive. When she first moved to Toronto from Jamaica as a young child, school was an escape from the domestic abuse she faced at home. At school, Palmer could be a regular child, socializing, playing sports and reading without repercussion. Looking back on her experiences now, however, she is disappointed her schools did not do more for her. School staff responded to signs of the abuse she was suffering with sympathy, not action. For years, she had prayed that her teachers would report her situation to the Children's Aid Society, but they never did. Despite these personal challenges, Palmer continued to thrive academically, completing high school, two college diplomas and a BA in modern languages.

When her children started school, her frustrations with the system reignited. In daycare, her first daughter had been appreciated as a lively, creative child, and was at the top of her class. But as soon as she entered formal schooling, Palmer was told that her daughter was badly behaved, wasn't learning and had a bad attitude. It turned out that her daughter had a learning disability, but it took considerable advocacy to have her assessed and provided with appropriate supports. The school seemed entirely unequipped to handle her, and Palmer felt judged and condescended to by the staff. Despite this, Palmer did her best to work with the teachers, and her daughter made it through school. The years when her teachers connected with her, she did well. The years when they didn't, she did not. Palmer did her best to advocate for her throughout, and to teach her daughter the skills she needed to advocate for herself.

Palmer did not want her son to experience the same difficulties her daughter had, and was clearly skeptical of what George Webster could offer him. Nancy volunteered to give Palmer a tour of the school, so she could form her own judgments about whether it would be a good fit for her son. It was only then that Nancy noticed Palmer's white cane—she was legally blind. She could read without difficulty, but had tunnel vision and limited depth perception. During the day, she could travel the city quite easily, but at night, she was almost totally blind, and relied upon others to get her from one place to another.

The tour started in front of the community bulletin boards where locals shared information about school and neighbourhood events. Next, they poked their heads into the double kindergarten classroom. While the educators interacted with small groups of students, a volunteer was sitting beside a little boy from North Korea, listening patiently as he read to her in halting English. Nancy helped Palmer down a short staircase to the ground-level hallway, where they came across a display created by one of the educational assistants to educate the larger community about autism and to advertise a monthly parent support group she had founded.

They then proceeded to the diagnostic kindergarten classroom, which was physically connected to a mainstream kindergarten class by shared play space, allowing the two groups to mingle and play. They passed a music class, decorated with instruments from all over the world, and a room where free adult ESL classes were offered. In the school library, Palmer was pleased to observe students and community members sharing the same space. A mother was helping a group of adult immigrants develop their computer skills; the group was supported by a settlement worker who was based at the school three days a week.

Just past the library was the industrial kitchen, where volunteers from the community—mostly parents, but not all—prepared a morning meal and a hot lunch for the students every day. Moms and dads from around the world worked together to prepare these healthy but inexpensive meals. There were occasional disagreements about the best way to cook rice. Some misunderstandings arose from cultural differences: Jamaican volunteers tended to be more direct than their Bangladeshi counterparts, and the salty humour of Canadian-born volunteers could make Pakistani volunteers uncomfortable. The school provided regular workshops, including cultural sensitivity training, to ensure everyone worked together efficiently and gained transferrable skills to add to their résumés.

As they turned the corner to another hallway, Palmer heard singing and laughing coming from a classroom. This was the Parenting Centre, where the school hosted parents with their very young children. As Palmer entered the room, she was met by the happy, multi-language chatter of about twenty parents, caregivers and their charges. There was a mixture of regulars—refugee mothers waiting to have their status recognized and be permitted to work, home daycare providers ensuring stimulation for their charges, grandparent caregivers seeking community connections—and casual users, too. The parenting worker Rosalie dished out hugs along with advice and support. In her role, she provided daily structured activities, but mostly encouraged the parents to self-organize and to play with their children and each other. Rosalie was often the first contact for parents at George Webster and liaised closely with the kindergarten teachers so that transition to the classroom was smooth.

Nancy told Palmer about a range of extracurriculars available—recreation programs offered on-site by Parks and Recreation, Scouts About, and the school's pride and joy, its new hockey team. The head caretaker and a group of teachers had rounded up donations of equipment and ice time to ensure this normally expensive sport could be offered for free. (Even after several of the George Webster students moved on to their next schools, they would return to help coach the team and to share their enthusiasm for the sport with kids encountering it for the first time.)

Palmer was impressed with the array of services and supports that were available for children and their families—and by the many ways that someone like her could make a valued contribution to the school. Sensing that interest, Nancy asked Palmer if she would be willing to join the school council. Palmer declined reluctantly, explaining that her vision made nighttime travel difficult. Nancy suggested the school could pay for taxis to and from meetings so that Palmer could attend.

Once her son was enrolled at George Webster, Palmer began using the Parenting Centre and volunteering at the school regularly. At first she helped out in the kitchen, and read with students who needed a little bit of extra attention. It was not uncommon to see her selling popcorn at recess or supervising a monthly movie night for families, and she even spearheaded a multicultural potluck, talent show and arts festival to celebrate Black History Month. As she learned how the school worked, she was able to advocate even more effectively for her children.

When the school council co-chair withdrew from the position, Nancy immediately asked Palmer to take over. In this position, Palmer worked closely with the staff to help build a council that offered built-in learning opportunities. She also became a core organizer for her school cluster's Parent Academy, remarking, "I loved being around like-minded people who were interested in learning and growing and improving their children's lives as much as possible."

Palmer's volunteer work at George Webster and in the Model Schools cluster ultimately led her to become the co-chair of the Toronto District School Board's Inner City Advisory Committee. She has drawn on her own experiences, and what she's seen of well-functioning community hub schooling, to mitigate the effects of poverty in inner-city schools.[*]

George Webster provided a pathway for an outstanding parent leader like Palmer to gain city-wide influence over schooling. Perhaps more importantly, it ensured that her son's needs were met, a process that was built on a close collaboration between his teacher and his mother. Palmer informed the teacher that her son thrived when he was able to form relationships, and the teacher listened, making it a priority to help him connect to other students. By the end of his first year, the boy had demonstrated remarkable progress, and the school determined that he was ready for mainstream classes. Palmer had some reservations— she worried her son would shut down again. But she trusted Nancy and she trusted her son's teacher. The school assured Palmer that supports would be built into the grade 1 classroom to play to his strengths. Palmer agreed, and was overjoyed to see her son manage well, even thrive, in the mainstream.

Interdisciplinary Partnerships
The Model Schools for Inner Cities had a mandate to be the hearts of their communities, and to work in partnership to support the social, emotional and physical needs of their students. A key element of this approach included the creation and

---

[*] Palmer recently became a municipal activist, joining the City of Toronto's Tenants First Advisory Panel as one of thirteen residents of community housing properties. This panel is working to create a plan for the implementation of 2016's Tenants First Report.

funding of a community support worker position—someone to nurture relationships between the school and its local community, and to support the engagement of the community in the school.

In most schools, school-community relationships are an unfunded priority, an add-on to the responsibility of teachers and principals. Research Kelly conducted for People for Education in 2012 showed that only 15 percent of elementary schools across Ontario had a staff member, other than the principal, with school-community liaison responsibilities. Of those, only 18 percent received any pay for this work—only about 3 percent of all schools, total.[3] As a result, school-community relationships tend to be patchy and shockingly rare. Fewer than 20 percent of elementary schools "often" connect with recreation services or libraries, and fewer than 10 percent "often" partner with mental health or medical services. Principals cited many roadblocks to connecting with social services. Teachers can't stop in the middle of teaching for meetings with other service providers. They often see their job as located in the classroom and school, not the broader community, and worry about requests that might interfere with preparation or school-based activities. Community agencies are often deterred by rules, regulations, fees and seemingly constant changes in personnel within schools, as well as their own resource constraints.

At George Webster there were bumps in the rollout of the school-community program. Finding the right community support worker for the school was a challenge. At one point, George Webster was assigned a worker who didn't speak the languages most common in the school, and it became much harder to connect to the parent community. The ideal candidate needed to be able to corral useful community resources and connect with others meaningfully in order to facilitate true school-community collaboration.

Despite these challenges, the school-community program at George Webster produced quick and significant results. One community support worker started a "parent ambassador" program that recruited representatives from different language groups to spread news about school events in people's first languages and communicate back concerns from the community. She also facilitated a partnership with Toronto Public Health that led to the first school-based program for parents on raising sexually healthy children. And she coordinated a school-wide family trip to an amusement park that would otherwise have been financially out of reach for George Webster's families.

Through conversations with parents and the community, the staff determined that hearing and vision testing was a critical student need that was too often going unmet. George Webster arranged for annual testing for students, and soon discovered that dozens of students needed glasses and several had profound hearing loss. To eliminate as many barriers as possible, follow-up services with audiologists and optometrists were arranged for students who required them, and glasses were dispensed right at the school. The program was hugely successful, and, over the course of several years, grew into a core element of the Model Schools initiative, adopted across its 150 schools.

Through the hearing and vision screening, the Model Schools team identified a problem plaguing the community: many students did not seem to have a consistent health care provider. Without regular medical supervision, health problems were going untreated, and follow-up on referrals from walk-in clinics and emergency rooms was difficult. The team wondered if families' access to health care could be boosted if services were offered right inside the schools children already attended. Parents and staff at George Webster were motivated by the prospect of bringing a pediatric clinic to their school. They formed a steering committee with representatives from different community agencies, including the Child Development Institute, to generate a plan for a school-based clinic that could support the physical and mental well-being of students and their families.

The need for mental health services was particularly pressing. In addition to the chronic stress that comes with poverty, many of George Webster's students were refugees who had experienced trauma. Nancy had spent more nights than she could count dealing with urgent child welfare concerns. Although many of the parents and educators requested that a psychiatrist be on-staff at the clinic, the expert steering committee recommended a preventative approach. They advised investing in teaching social and emotional skills to all students (see Chapter 4) and developing a few specialized mental health programs, like play therapy. The school's partnership with specialized mental health agencies and professionals, and the proactive strategies it developed through their guidance, ultimately converted student mental health from a major worry into a point of pride in the school.

By funding its medical expenses, the Ministry of Health covered the health clinic's greatest expenses, but George Webster still faced major costs not funded by provincial health insurance or by the Model Schools funding. For example, the school wanted to hire a clinic coordinator to provide administrative support, and had to pay workers to set up the clinic space. The school and steering committee wound up having to fundraise,* and succeeded in reaching donors well beyond the neighbourhood. The school raised almost seventy-five thousand dollars, and in March 2011,

---

* School fundraising makes inequity visible. In Toronto, the wealthiest schools often easily raise over two hundred thousand dollars, whereas the poorest are lucky to raise a few thousand. Yet the schools with the lowest fundraising capacity are of course the ones in which large-scale investments, if managed effectively, could make the biggest difference. See Chapter 7.

George Webster opened the doors of the Dr. Paul Steinhauer Pediatric Clinic.

The clinic currently serves over twenty schools, and has approximately 1,300 children and infants registered as patients. Although it only operates one day a week, it has helped to keep students at school and healthy. The number of students suspended for missed vaccinations has been reduced by 80 percent, and immunity has improved for the whole community. The clinic has also significantly improved access to health care for refugee families, many new to the neighbourhood and especially in need of help. On an individual level, Nancy remembers one student who struggled to concentrate in class. When the teacher-librarian investigated, she realized the girl was incredibly itchy due to bedbug bites. She was able to receive treatment at the school clinic that very afternoon, missing only a few minutes of class time instead of the hours she likely would have waited at a drop-in clinic (if she was brought in for treatment at all).

George Webster's pediatric clinic helped to establish best practices for the Model Schools initiative, and when the clinic proved its worth, the program spread. Today, there are seven clinics in schools across Toronto.

George Webster's approach to being a community hub involved bringing as many services as possible directly into the school. This model made sense, given the school's geography and demographics—but it is not the only way to ensure that students have access to the full range of services and supports they need.

St. Stephen Middle School is another school that is notable for its engagement with its community. Located in St. Stephen, a small town in the southwest corner of New Brunswick, the middle school houses 340 students in grades 6 through 8. As recently retired principal Alan Dunfield (another one of Canada's Outstanding Principals) describes it, the school includes students from "both ends of the rainbow and all points in-between." Culturally, the school is quite homogeneous, but students come from a range of socio-economic backgrounds, and some face significant challenges including poverty. "We have kids who come in and this is the happy part of their day. We don't know what they did the night before and what the night before did to them," he says.

To serve the whole child and provide as many opportunities as possible, the school works with its community through an effective, agile system of needs assessment and referral. St. Stephen was one of the first schools in the province to pilot this program, developed by the provincial government. As with British Columbia's development and implementation of performance standards for social responsibility (Chapter 3), the Government of New Brunswick was compelled to take action based on intensive self-reflection in the wake of a teen's tragic and preventable death. In 2007, nineteen-year-old Ashley Smith died in prison while guards stood by and watched her strangle herself. Ruled a homicide after an extensive inquest, her death was widely acknowledged to also reflect failures of the system, with an ill-equipped criminal justice system taking the place of comprehensive mental health services.[4]

The Government of New Brunswick subsequently developed a blueprint to "reduce the risk, address the need."[5] It was clear that a preventative approach had to go beyond criminal justice or even mental health services. Ultimately, the blueprint involved four government departments—education, health, police and welfare institutions—working together to address the needs of vulnerable children. Bob Eckstein, the director of integrated services delivery for New Brunswick, sees schools as the centre of this initiative. In an integrated, preventative response to mental health problems, schools must be the link between families and services.

At St. Stephen Middle School, this translates into a team consisting of school leadership and student support staff, as well as a new integrated services delivery representative. The team meets every Monday to address issues of mental health, safety and wellness brought to their attention by the teachers. They make decisions about whether there are more school-based strategies they can try, or whether they need help from the outside. On Tuesdays, the integrated services delivery representative meets with a group that includes mental health and social development specialists, the RCMP, regional health authorities, the school district office, clinical psychologists and probation officers in order to partner students with the services they need. When different agencies work through a problem together, students receive a coordinated response. And the turnaround between identifying a problem and delivering the requisite services is remarkably quick. Best of all, many of the services can be provided right in the school.

To illustrate the power of St. Stephen's approach, Dunfield shared the story of Sam. Sam had an average year in grade 6, but in grade 7, he began to spiral. He started leaving school without permission and skipping classes. He insisted that everyone hated him and he threatened to kill himself. Teachers, the guidance counsellor and the administration all tried to work with him but were unable to give him the highly specialized help he needed. Ultimately, they referred him to the integrated services team.

The team paired Sam with a social worker, Truly Urquart, who immediately addressed one of largest challenges in helping Sam— the distrust between Sam's parents and the school staff. Sam, in his suffering, had been telling his parents that the school staff was unkind and working against his best interests. Understandably, his parents were frustrated and concerned. As a third party, Urquart mediated conversations between the parents and the school, and ensured all were working together to find a solution. As she explained it, "Everyone has different information, but we're all on 'Team Sam.'"

With improved trust and relationships, Sam's parents finally accepted a recommendation to have him clinically assessed by a psychiatrist—one of the integrated services team's strongest recommendations. Sam was diagnosed with generalized anxiety disorder, which enabled his doctor, family and school to create a specific treatment plan tailored to his needs. Urquart taught Sam to identify the triggers for his anxiety and deal with them appropriately, and Sam began to meet with the school guidance counsellor every morning to set a positive tone for the rest of the day. Urquart also negotiated a special timetable for Sam, designed to subdue his anxiety. Sam attended only those courses he was doing well in, and saw a tutor for every other subject. This schedule set Sam up for success, eliminating factors that proved debilitating and allowing him to cultivate confidence in his abilities.

At first, Sam came in to school for just half the day. As his achievement rose and his anxiety diminished, he began to stay at school for lunch, eating in a private setting with a close friend instead of in the cafeteria, where he felt self-conscious. Soon, he was attending classes after lunch as well.

In most schools, it is likely that Sam, threatening suicide and leaving the premises without permission, would have been suspended indefinitely for his own safety and the safety of others. Urquart equates the integrated services approach to one-stop shopping, in stark contrast to the string of the referrals often typical in the child welfare system. When strategy after ineffective strategy is proposed, families lose trust in the system and children go untreated. Thanks to the integrated services model, which brought the school, Sam's parents and a variety of experts together, Sam was assigned a thoughtful strategy that worked quickly and in a coordinated way.

Bob Eckstein reports that integrated services teams are now in two school districts, strengthening their preventative and intervention strategies as they work with more and more children. Based on its early success, the government has committed to spreading the project across New Brunswick by 2018.

Serving the Community

A school can be a powerful presence in a community, shaping it much as it shapes its students.

The anglophone schools of Quebec have turned this notion into a well-researched educational model, and have applied it to great effect.

A decade ago, Paule Langevin, a former teacher working at the Ministry of Education, observed that francophone communities in the rest of Canada received funding, funnelled through schools, to support community development. She started to ask why anglophone communities in Quebec did not receive the same. Convinced that involving families and communities in schools was the best way to support these linguistic-minority students, she approached Heritage Canada with a proposal to create anglophone Community Learning Centres (CLCs) across Quebec. She envisioned schools that could bolster their communities by offering the services they needed. Her request was granted, and fifteen schools across the province were selected to become CLCs, receiving forty thousand dollars in annual funding each.

Every CLC was assigned a community liaison worker, whose responsibilities included convening ongoing local partnership tables that allowed the principal and local community groups—from public health and food security agencies to business organizations—to meet. Together, the schools and these groups conducted needs-and-gap assessments to determine where common interests lay and how they could align services. The community liaison person then sought grants, on average raising twice the value of their salaries.

The CLC program has faced its share of hurdles. Because of the nature of the funding, there have always been two sets of goals for the CLCs: the federal government looks for outcomes that enhance community vitality, whereas the provincial government is seeking outcomes reflecting student success. Limited resources have posed another challenge. There are always more schools interested in becoming CLCs than there are funds. And convincing teachers to take on additional work has required some effort. Langevin, now the CLC initiative director, remarked: "Schools act like they don't want to have anything to do with community, but the community wanted access to the schools, to the students, to provide services that they were mandated to deliver. Often, it is like when schools say they want to work with parents, it's true, but only on their own terms."

Nevertheless, over the decade, the CLCs have come to embody different forms. Most schools offer some sort of early childhood programming. Many emphasize lifelong learning for adults in the community. One school in middle-class Magog, Quebec, runs several community night school sessions a year, where in addition to learning, everyone is expected to take a turn teaching—anything from cooking to small motor repair to literature. A school in a depressed area of Montreal has found funds to keep its playground open and staffed after hours, and has established a community garden in partnership with the municipality and a local seniors' centre. Seniors who hadn't set foot in the school since they graduated fifty or more years ago now maintain the garden alongside the high school students.

By 2014–2015, only nine years after launching, the thirty-seven CLCs across Quebec boasted more than two thousand partnership agreements with local, regional, provincial and national organizations. Through their collaborative work, these partners have leveraged more than ten million dollars of in-kind services and resources to serve their schools and communities—an average return on investment of 2.84 relative to the cost of staffing the position in each school.[6]

The Quebec CLCs, in almost all cases, are thriving. Anglophone parents now report that they are choosing to send their children to CLCs because they are vibrant places where things are happening. Previously, even parents who had been educated in English themselves, and were therefore allowed to enrol their children in English education under Bill 101, had often perceived the French schools to be better resourced and more attractive. Langevin believes her staff has "really shaken up" anglophone communities, elevating their services and bringing people together. Anglophone schools are now better able to connect to provincial resources, sitting at the big community table alongside francophone schools.

There is evidence of improved student academic success, too. Results from a well-established student survey called "Tell Them From Me," suggest that students from CLCs work harder, do more homework, miss less school and have higher aspirations for post-secondary education than those in similarly situated schools across Canada. CLC students were also more likely to be involved in clubs and sports outside gym class, and more likely to report that they liked school. When schools form meaningful connections with their communities, and give back to them, students and families benefit.

John Jerome Paul, introduced in Chapter 1, also views children's education as inextricably linked to the larger community. Early in his career, before he became Mi'kmaw Kina'matnewey (MK)'s director of programs, Paul was as an adult educator. The year was 1990, and he had been charged with running an "adult upgrading" course in Eskasoni, the largest Mi'kmaw community (population 3,400). "It was a fifteen-week course to transition into the workforce," he remembers, "but into low-paying jobs that weren't even available in the community. It was crazy. We were twenty-five miles away from any jobs— 'upgrade' into what?"

Eskasoni's adults were being trained in low-paying fields that neither existed in their community nor met their needs, and their children were suffering accordingly. What the community needed were nurses and teachers. Paul understood that by offering real opportunities for educational enrichment, he could help to strengthen the whole community. He transformed the short-term "upgrading" course into a night school that prepared adult students for university, and "not a job at Tim Hortons." He focused on literacy, numeracy, conducting research and using computers.

Under his leadership, the Training and Education Centre flourished, with thirty-four programs operating at one time, including day school, night school, weekend programs, March break and summer holiday programs, adult literacy courses in English and Mi'kmaq, GED and college programs, university courses, distance education and even drivers' ed. Paul remembers with delight a student in a grade 9 school re-entry program finding himself studying beside his middle school vice-principal.

"What are you doing here?" the student asked.

"Working on my master's," replied his teacher.

Suddenly, Paul's thirty- to fifty-year-old graduates were going on to university. And as their university enrolment rose, the Mi'kmaw communities began to have an influence on programming in their local higher-learning institutions, Cape Breton University (CBU) and St. Francis Xavier. Alongside the Board of Governors at CBU, they challenged all departments to find ways of incorporating Indigenous knowledge into their courses. Life Sciences was the first program to accept the challenge, attending an MK lecture by renowned ethno-botanical geneticist Dr. Gregory Cajete, and introducing a new course on Indigenous medicinal botany to run at both CBU and at the Training and Education Centre.

The university graduates were bringing their skills home too. One university cohort was made up exclusively of young single mothers—including Paul's own daughter. Their program of study was also science, and from that group emerged three registered nurses, two teachers and a principal who all came back to work in Mi'kmaw communities.

The active adult education strategy has brought about a transformation in the communities' education culture. Paul remarked upon the enthusiasm for learning that has flowed from adults to children: "Everybody is in on it." Compared to twenty years ago, when Paul was one of only two Indigenous educators, MK now reports that 80 percent of its staff is Indigenous, and most principals are Mi'kmaw.

Building community into schools—and building schools into the community—is important for youth, especially the most vulnerable among them. Schools simply cannot do it alone. When they partner with parents, local specialists and services, and the wider community, they can offer their students a holistic approach to education that can be modified to meet any need. And when schools offer their services outward, they can help to spread a culture of learning; by educating a community, they support its children in aiming higher.

The schools we visited in this chapter are schools of the future, and their successes align with the three principles Nancy's father emphasized years ago: the importance of early "upstream" intervention; the benefits born from interdisciplinary, team-based strategies; and the centrality of family and community to a child's achievement and wellness.

Applying these principles has required two kinds of system changes: first, an acceptance that schools must be responsible for more than students' academic achievement, and second, meaningful financial investments in school-community engagement. The extent to which schools take on the mission to support their communities, and are enabled to do so both financially and through well integrated community resources, will be one of the key litmus tests of future educational excellence.

SEVEN

THE CHILDREN WE SHARE

"The way that schools care about children is reflected in the way schools care about the children's families. If educators view children simply as students they are likely to see the family as separate from school. If educators view students as children, they are likely to see both the family and the community as partners with the school in children's education and development."

—JOYCE EPSTEIN,
"School/Family/Community Partnerships"[1]

P arents and educators are *most often* united by a shared desire for what's best for children. Both feel pride when children make progress, overcome obstacles and reach their goals. Teachers and parents can offer meaningful support to each other. Or they can be each other's sharpest critics, with anger and judgment to spare. When parents feel heard and teachers feel respected, extraordinary things can happen. This isn't always as easy as it sounds—misalignment of values, missteps in communication, and significant cultural or socioeconomic differences are hard to bridge without a healthy dose of mutual regard and understanding.

In Ontario, parental involvement is actually mandated. Ontario Regulation 612 requires that every school have a school council, and that the majority of its members, including the chair, must be parents. It defines the council's purpose as "through the active participation of parents, to improve pupil achievement and to enhance the accountability of the education system to parents."

The Challenge of Enacting Change
Dewson Street Public School, Kelly's children's downtown Toronto public elementary school, holds six hundred students from junior kindergarten to grade 6. The school is in a neighbourhood that has

been rapidly gentrifying. It encompasses a fairly diverse group of families, including long-time Italian and Portuguese residents and relatively new English-language learners, as well as being home to considerable economic diversity. Whereas the dominant group of parents at Dewson are relatively affluent downtown dwellers, about 15 percent of families live on incomes of less than thirty thousand dollars. For five years, Kelly was the secretary and co-chair of the school council and experienced first-hand how rewarding—and challenging—participating in schools as a parent can be. While the council produced tangible results, members struggled with the limitations of what they could accomplish. Often, the council's influence on the school felt more like a performance than reality. By and large school councils are expected to keep their focus on whole-school and extracurricular issues and *off* what students are doing in their classrooms.

Kelly's council experience was often marked by virulent debates that raised big issues but had small practical stakes. Kelly has vivid memories of multi-year battles around, for example, whether kids should get medals for cross-country running. Some parents were in favour of medals, in order to tempt less-willing kids to get active; others thought the medals would detract from the intrinsic rewards of physical activity. Still others were upset by the suggestion that school council funds should cover the cost of medals when there were more urgent needs to address. This topic, which seems inoffensive on the surface, came up every year, and every year angry emails flew.

Other council debates grew heated because they brought political differences to light. When the council discussed whether it should allow a fee-paying chess club to operate during the school day, it pitted those who saw chess as an important intellectual exercise against those who believed that school-day activities should be available without financial barriers. This matter, too, took several years to resolve, and involved countless acrimonious meetings. (Ultimately, the council settled on a paid after-school program, preserving the principle of a fee-free school day.)

The low-stakes nature of these debates reflects the limited role of school councils, which is, to some degree, a matter of design. The system favours the permanent and full-time players: teachers, administrators and board members. When Kelly was a board member at her children's daycare, she was involved in matters of far greater urgency and importance to the institution. She assisted with the managing of staff, determined what kids should eat (and how to make their food safe) and wrestled with how to balance the endlessly tight budget. By contrast, the running of the school is mostly managed by professionals—offering parents far richer institutional resources, like the guarantee of qualified staff who routinely receive professional development, yet far less influence. The closest most school councils get to shaping a school's core business is by making recommendations to the principal. At Kelly's school council meetings, the parents regularly grilled the principal on a range of issues—a monthly ritual that required considerable diplomacy from the principal but rarely provided parents with the satisfaction of affecting fundamental change.

It is indisputable that Dewson's parents contributed to a richer school culture, stronger parent networks and a wider range of experiences for students than could have been provided by staff alone. Yet the observation of a Dewson parent who is a teacher at another school is also true: educators often perceive school councils as "just want want want," and tend to be quite skeptical of parental demands for change. From the school's perspective, dealing with parents can involve juggling a wide range of often inconsistent demands. The reality is that parents don't speak with one voice—and rarely does the loudest voice speak for all. And in the midst of contention, schools must ensure too that the needs of the system are fulfilled, from following the curriculum to ensuring financial, safety and human rights requirements are met.

Parents vs. the System: Sex Ed in Thorncliffe Park

Perhaps nowhere has the conflict between the system and parents been more visible than in the struggle over Ontario's new health curriculum.

Until 2015, Ontario schools had been teaching a health curriculum that was developed in the 1990s and included almost no information about cyber safety, newly prevalent drugs like crystal meth and opioids, nor about sexual orientation and gender identity. In 2010, the provincial government attempted an update but withdrew its revised curriculum following only a few days of widespread news coverage of a protest planned by Evangelist Christian minister Charles McVety and supported by the Catholic bishops, among others. Over the next few years, a group of fifty organizations, including public health authorities, advocated for the timely implementation of a new curriculum. Their polling suggested that 93 percent of Ontario parents wanted students to learn current, accurate information about sex and human development at school.[2] Finally, under the leadership of Premier Kathleen Wynne, an updated health curriculum was released in the spring of 2015.

Ironically, Wynne's new curriculum faced its fiercest resistance in Thorncliffe Park, a neighbourhood in Don Valley West, where she serves as MPP. When Thorncliffe Park was designed in the 1950s, planners anticipated that its tall apartment towers would house twelve thousand people; today, with thirty thousand residents, it boasts the highest population density in Canada. The neighbourhood has become a landing place for new immigrants from all over the world, primarily Pakistan, the Philippines and Afghanistan. Three quarters of households are families with children (compared to two thirds, city-wide); by national standards, almost 40 percent of residents live in overcrowded housing. Despite levels of post-secondary education on par with the city as a whole, the rate of unemployment is double.

The early underestimate of its population has had a lasting impact on services and schools in the area. With 1,310 students enrolled in the 2015–2016 school year, Thorncliffe Park Public School is the largest elementary school in the Toronto District School Board (TDSB). On the same street, a brand-new kindergarten school, the Fraser Mustard Early Learning Academy, houses another 650 kids in junior and senior kindergarten. And down the road, Valley Park Middle School serves 950 children in grades 6, 7 and 8.

Eid Ismaili is a Thorncliffe Park resident who was opposed to the new curriculum. He lives in a six-storey co-op with his wife, an Egyptian-trained lawyer, and their two Canadian-born sons, who attend Valley Park Middle School and Thorncliffe Park Public School. Blind since he was forty days old, Ismaili came to Canada in his early twenties to escape the war in South Sudan. He is now studying human rights at York University, and he performs as a singer at Sudanese, Ethiopian and Eritrean weddings around Toronto. In the last provincial election, he was an active supporter of Premier Kathleen Wynne. He explained, "I used to be best friends with Kathleen. I used to introduce her to the community, share ideas." He paused. "I feel sorry, now."

In March 2015, Ismaili received a phone call from a member of the school council. The council was hosting a meeting to discuss the new health curriculum. Intrigued, Ismaili attended. "I went. I am a father, I have kids and I wanted to know," he said. There, he encountered information that distressed him. The new curriculum, he was told, would teach young children about sex and masturbation in highly explicit terms. Ismaili does not want his children to be exposed to any form of sex education at school, believing it should be parents' responsibility to teach their children about this sensitive subject. "Yes, you need a lesson about this," he says, "you need to be careful with your friend, your fiancé, with others in society. But for us, we train from home." The reason he moved to Canada was because of its protection of freedom of speech and religion: "I chose to be here because Canadians respect democracy, and I believe if you want to practise your freedom of thought, assembly, speech, it is in Canada you can do so," he explained.

He was not the only parent who was deeply concerned. The Thorncliffe Parents Association soon formed, a loosely organized group that vociferously opposed the new curriculum. They spread information about the curriculum via email and Facebook, in English, Arabic and Urdu, often sensationally misrepresenting it by excerpting teacher prompts out of context. The curriculum included *suggested* responses to student questions, such as this reply to a grade 6 student who asks about masturbation: "Exploring one's body by touching or masturbating is something that many people do and find pleasurable. It is common and not harmful and one way of learning about your body." The *Toronto Star* obtained an anonymous letter in Arabic that told parents that grade 1 students would be exposed to images of private parts and taught to touch their own. In grade 6, they would be shown how to masturbate, and in grade 8, they would receive instruction on anal sex play. "In the Making Sex Feel Good unit, they will be asked to look at sexy magazines and movies to investigate what arouses and seduces them."[3] These assertions, of course, were entirely fabricated.

"What floored me more than the flyers was that people believed them," said Jeff Crane, the principal of Thorncliffe Park.

An energetic leader in his mid-forties, he describes the best part of his job as "the pure adrenalin of making everything that has to happen, go." With more than 1,300 students, Crane can't know them all by name—but they know him. As Kelly followed him through the halls, some kids approached shyly to say hello, others asked to go to the bathroom. He was introduced to the proud father of two Roma girls registering at the school; the family had spent that morning with an ESL specialist to get them into the system. Before the new curriculum was introduced, Crane and his team had offered accommodations in the teaching of sex and sexuality at the school, out of respect for its large Muslim population. As a matter of equality rights, and as required by the school board, all children learned about a range of family structures and sexual orientations at different points in the curriculum. But boys and girls were taught the health curriculum around sex ed separately, and in less explicit terms than might occur in other schools. A small number of parents would exercise the right to have their children "opt out" of particular classes. With the introduction of the new curriculum, however, Crane found himself squarely in the middle of a maelstrom that attracted national and even international attention. The new curriculum created harder lines about what was required learning—and nobody was happy with minor adjustments. After a public meeting was shut down in Scarborough because of loud and competing protests, Crane was advised to hold off on engaging with dissenting parents.

In the meantime, activist parents from Thorncliffe were mobilizing. They partnered with Campaign Life Coalition, a national anti-abortion organization, and Canadian Families Alliance, another parent group formed in opposition to the curriculum. With these mostly Christian groups, they held marches from the Ontario Legislature down Toronto's University Avenue, and they began planning a province-wide strike around the demand that all sex-related material be removed from the education curriculum. On the day of the strike, 35,000 students were kept home from school. Although publicized across the province, Thorncliffe was the apex of the protest. At the elementary school, 1,220 out of 1,350 students were not in class, and hundreds of protesters congregated outside the school.

Ismaili did not join the Thorncliffe Parents Association, but he was an active part of the strike, gathering outside the school and speaking to the media. "The thing that made me really protest—I feel the kids have to enjoy their lives as kids. You can't tell kids, 'go and have the desire because you are ready for it right now.' If a person is not grown up yet, to me, this is criminal," he said. By the time the curriculum was set to be rolled out in September, Ismaili had resolved not to send his boys back to school. Instead, he was one of many parents who sent their children to Thorncliffe Park's "school under the trees," a volunteer-run home-schooling effort in the community.

Crane did hear from some parents that they wanted to send their kids to school but were afraid to. Some began bringing their children in an hour late to avoid the protestors. On day two of the new curriculum, the words "SHAME ON YOU" were graffitied on the school, leading to accusations from both sides, but neither took responsibility. Crane began to receive disturbing letters from people across Canada and beyond, insisting the protestors should "go back to their own country" or "adapt to *our* culture." Despite the fact that multiple faith groups, including Catholics and Evangelical Christians, were working together to oppose the new curriculum, Thorncliffe Park's large Muslim population received the most attention—and almost all the backlash. As tensions rose, with support from the board, the school began employing security guards at the beginning and end of the day.

By October, the protest groups had begun to fracture. Some

members of the Thorncliffe Parents Association began to distribute explicitly homophobic materials about Premier Wynne's "homosexual indoctrine" [sic], which was deeply offensive to many. Others condemned "so-called Community partners" like Public Health and Planned Parenthood being brought in to schools to teach children about health and sexuality: "Should we allow those beasts to come and feast on our kids?" one controversial Facebook post asked.[4] It soon became clear that not all the local parents were happy with this tack. Although Ismaili had protested the new curriculum in September, and had subsequently chosen to home-school his children, he found it "really hard" to witness the parents' more aggressive tactics. He distanced himself from the rhetoric. "If you are eighteen years old, you have the right to be what you want to be. I have to judge myself first before others," he said.

Around this time, Ismaili began looking for an alternative to "the school under the trees." The home-schooling endeavour would not be sustainable in winter, volunteers needed to find paying work and parents were growing concerned that they would lose social assistance if their kids did not attend school. Ismaili and his wife decided to enrol their children at the Seerah Mission School, a Muslim school that promises "excellence in academics, excellence in character."

At Thorncliffe Park, Crane began reaching out to parents to discuss the new curriculum. Between October and November, he held twenty evening sessions open to parents only, with more than 650 attending overall, three classes at a time. These sessions required a major time commitment, but according to Crane, "Since this was taking up all my time anyway, I thought we might as well do it on my terms." The conversations helped the parents and Crane alike: "I got to see that our parents are concerned parents like anybody else—they wanted to know what their children were learning. Not all left happy, but they were respectful and appreciative," he said, "It is easy to get caught up in the moment, to think all these parents are ignorant. That certainly wasn't the case."

Using these conversations and the school board's religious accommodation binder for guidance, the school created an adjusted, optional health curriculum. Forty percent of grade 1 parents, for example, opted for an accommodated safety lesson in which the term "private parts," and not the names of male and female genitalia, is used. The purpose of the lesson is to teach children that nobody should touch their genitalia, and that message is clearly conveyed to both groups of students. The school continues to teach the broader curriculum, including respect for the equality rights of gays and lesbians and diverse families.

But this accommodation itself became controversial. One group of sex education advocates argued on the radio that children are put at risk of child abuse if they aren't taught the names of genitalia; another expert went on the record to insist that "the accommodations met the spirit of the curriculum." Some other schools that had taken a different approach received renewed pressure from parents to offer an accommodated curriculum. Eventually, this tempest settled, the minister of education going on the record to state that Thorncliffe Park's modifications were a reasonable accommodation of religious beliefs.

During this time, Ismaili's sons began to ask if they could go back to their old schools. The oldest boy, a thoughtful child with a shy smile, told Kelly that he wished Seerah Mission School had a library, and that he missed his friends. Ismaili, too, began to have concerns. Among his classmates at York, he had met a number of graduates of religious schools—Islamic and Christian alike—and he thought it was a challenge for them to live among those who did not share their beliefs. When he observed the Seerah Mission School's strong emphasis on the Qur'an, and on

Arabic instruction instead of French, he feared the school was not preparing his children "to live anywhere in the world" and understand other people. He explained, "I want them to be educated in their religion, to be good people, whatever they want to be, but to be able to work in the bigger world. We are all in this society, we have to share what we have."

Ismaili decided to visit the principal at Valley Park Middle School to voice his concerns. After the meeting, he wrote two letters to the school. One letter was a formal request that his son be exempted from sexual health education classes, because he wanted to be their "first educator" in this subject. The school agreed to his "opting out": parents' rights in that regard had not changed. Most students in the school were taught the curriculum, which includes content on delaying sex, consent and decision making, STD prevention, contraception and gender identity; Ismaili's were not. The other letter was a thank-you note, because "they accepted my need, and they helped my child to be in the school." He sent the same letters to Crane at Thorncliffe Park, and then he re-enrolled his boys. When Kelly asked Ismaili's son if his classmates did anything special on his first day back, he replied, "They just welcomed me." He had a long list of things he likes about his school: his friends, his teacher, science and social studies classes, and getting to meet children's author Deborah Ellis at a book festival. His father is pleased that his children are back at Thorncliffe Park and Valley Park, too. He must have found five different ways to say that he understands how difficult educators' roles are, caught between their obligation to serve both the government and parents.

Why did the protests against the new health curriculum become so virulent in Thorncliffe Park? Some of the huge interest in the Thorncliffe Park dispute reflected the notion that there is a fundamental incommensurability between cultures, though the experiences of Jeff Crane, a white, non-Muslim man working in the community, and Eid Ismaili, a proudly Muslim human rights activist, suggest a more nuanced dynamic.

Some structural factors in Thorncliffe Park also contributed to the uprising. The high population density in the neighbour-hood means that families with nascent cultural connections to Canada and high socio-economic needs are being served in the city's largest schools. Research conducted in Chicago indicates that it is much easier to build bonds of trust between schools and their surrounding communities when schools are small, with approximately three hundred students.[5] Conflict resolution, in particular, is much easier to negotiate in a smaller school. The de-escalation of conflicts around the new health curriculum happened at smaller schools away from the public's eye—in edu-cator–parent conversations, a few classes at a time. But it was not just the size of the school population that worked against more peaceful, trusting engagement. The fact that Thorncliffe's students must contend with extra transitions—attending three schools between kindergarten and grade 8—makes it even more difficult for parents to form strong connections to schools. The larger politics of educational and municipal decision making were invisible in how the battle lines were drawn, but the under-lying questions of who gets heard and how resources are allo-cated were deeply implicated in the drama at Thorncliffe Park.

Parent activism around the health curriculum is an example of parents enacting tangible change in schools. It is also an example of how larger forces can make that process a thorny one. Some of the material produced by the Thorncliffe Parents Association, Campaign Life and others went well beyond advo-cating for children, and included homophobic lies. Identities mattered—the Muslim face of the dispute made a difference, and Premier Wynne's sexuality made her a particular target.

Nevertheless, parents should be vocal advocates for their children, and schools should be prepared to accommodate them. Through their protests, parents of Thorncliffe Park made their voices heard, but it was through the spirit of co-operation and respect between Jeff Crane and parents like Eid Ismaili that the most productive change was affected. It is a credit to both parents and educators that the structural factors were, ultimately, not insurmountable: At the end of the 2015–2016 school year, the enrolment at Thorncliffe was back up to 1,310 students, down only 40 students from the year before.

Parents Getting Political: Schools Welcome Refugees

One of Kelly's most rewarding experiences, as part of a school and national community, was a large-scale, parent-led movement to enact change beyond the walls of the school, through engaging school communities in refugee sponsorship and support.

On Labour Day weekend in the fall of 2015 (just as the controversy over the health curriculum was blistering at Thorncliffe Park), a boat full of refugees fleeing the Syrian civil war capsized in the Mediterranean. Three-year-old Alan Kurdi's body was photographed on the beach, and suddenly the ongoing Syrian crisis had a human face.

Kelly had wanted to sponsor a refugee family, but the commitment was considerable. According to government estimations, sponsorship costs hosts approximately thirty thousand dollars to sponsor a family of four, and requires them to go through a complex and lengthy application process that in September 2015 was expected to take fifty-two months. In the 1970s, when fifty thousand Vietnamese refugees escaped to Canada, the most common way for middle-class Canadians to help had been through churches and other religious organizations. Neither Kelly nor most of her friends were members of active religious communities, but

Kelly could think of another institution through which people come together as a community.

In today's world, schools are a key site for the creation of social capital. The well-being of children is at the centre of a school's adult community; a healthy dose of idealism or altruism is therefore already a vital part of parents' and teachers' connection to one another. For this reason, Kelly believed that her school community would be capable of, and interested in, supporting a family from across the world. She suspected others would be moved by a desire to assist the vulnerable and show their children how to remake the world.

On the second day of school, Kelly went to speak to Dewson's principal, Janice Robinson, to explain that she and three other parents wanted to start a group at the school to sponsor a refugee family as a community. Robinson wept at the idea, and, subject to an okay from the school council, gave the project a green light. Kelly emailed the executive of the school council that afternoon, and received a response from the outgoing chair, D. Williams, within a few hours. Williams cautioned that the undertaking was ambitious, noted they would need buy-in from the school board and stressed the importance of ensuring this was a valuable learning experience for students, then wrote: "The issues in Syria are huge . . . but if it is possible to save one family from that horrific situation, save that family."

Kelly's group shared their goal on the school's Facebook page, and their numbers began to grow. They distributed a survey to Dewson's parents to canvass support and ideas, and within thirty-six hours, 298 of the school's 400 families had responded. In total, 83 percent supported the idea of a school sponsorship. A few people questioned whether sponsorship should really be the work of a school, but some of them wanted to donate regardless. An informal check-in with the staff revealed that even though work-to-rule was in effect, they would stand behind parents taking this initiative.

Calling themselves Schools Welcome Refugees, the organizing group launched the fundraising campaign with a letter to parents, a website and a press conference. Their initial goal was to raise thirty thousand dollars in thirty days, but, to help publicize the initiative, they decided to challenge other schools to join in. Kelly knew that not all of Canada's fifteen thousand schools would want to take on the challenge, but guessed that, perhaps, one in fifteen would. The 1000 School Challenge was born.

The first press conference was sparsely attended, but CTV ran a story featuring interviews with students about why it was important to help refugees now. The pledge envelopes went out, and Kelly's group held their breath to see if they would meet their goal. A buzz began to build. CBC sent a journalist to film a fundraising lemonade stand organized by a group of children in grades 4 and up.

In those very first days, more than a dozen schools accepted Dewson's challenge of sponsoring a refugee family. Kelly went into the school office at the end of the first week of the campaign to find the staff humming with excitement. They had received a one-thousand-dollar donation from a stranger moved by the idea of children trying to help refugees. "I've never seen *anything* like this," said Jennifer Brodie, Dewson's dedicated office manager. Dewson's teachers had been speaking to their students about the crisis, and a *Globe and Mail* columnist wrote an article on the students' perspectives on refugees. The students were struck by the tragedy, and saw a need to get involved. Eleven-year-old Mahta Amini explained, "You see an innocent person die and you feel you want to get involved. You don't want to see another innocent person die for nothing just because they don't want to be in a war and get hurt. I think Canada should do something about it." Asked why Canadians should get involved with refugees, her classmate Hannah Hewko explained simply "It's a global crisis." The Canadian government's response to the Syrian crisis, at that time, was still based on distancing and fear, and the media coverage of Dewson helped to change the conversation. As the columnist wrote, the voices of children brought unmistakable moral clarity to the issue.

The Dewson group had asked that pledge envelopes be returned two weeks into their campaign, so that they would have time to organize other fundraising events if they fell short of their goal. The organizing group, which had continued to grow, sat around a dining room table, tallying donations from over six hundred individuals. Some of the pledge envelopes were full of money that was literally sticky, having come from bake sales and lemonade stands. Kelly still has the final tally, with a heart around the number: $31,208. She can vividly remember the feeling of blood leaving her face when she realized they had reached their goal.

Principal Robinson and the school staff gathered the students for an assembly to celebrate that achievement and to learn more about the issues behind the action. The assembly was a learning experience all around. At least one educator at the school was worried that the subject would be too upsetting for the children. What no one expected was that several students, very young ones, would put up their hands to share their own families' experiences of fleeing conflict or persecution. A little boy, who seemed to be about seven, popped his hand up to share his parents' stories of hiding in a cupboard to escape the army in the Bosnian War. Another grade 4 student explained that her grandparents had fled Chile after the military coup led by General Augusto Pinochet. "My grandparents had a hard time but they are here now. I feel really good that we are raising money for another family that needs it," she explained to a *Globe and Mail* reporter.[6]

As Kelly worked with other schools from across the country, she came to appreciate the strong collaboration that enabled the Dewson team to achieve their goal. Ultimately, about forty schools got involved with different action projects or sponsorships. A handful had overwhelmingly positive experiences, like Dewson's, but many faced challenges that Dewson had not. A number of parents wrote in to say that their children's schools simply didn't have the fundraising capacity for a sponsorship. Other schools did not have a working infrastructure promoting communication with parents. Even more schools had leaders who were nervous about the initiative, about being too political on a controversial issue or undertaking a new and ill-defined responsibility for staff.

The novelty and size of the initiative were a worry for the TDSB, too. With so many schools raising huge amounts of money, the systemic urge for oversight kicked in. As is often the case, the first response to anything risky—even to a project they consider worthy—was to shut it down, and Schools Welcome Refugees *was* risky. There was no protection in place against fraud—Dewson had relied upon trust, but "the system" needed rules. Ultimately, the project acquired enough attention and momentum that the board's associate director of finance and operations, Carla Kisko, stepped in to encourage the business office to develop more workable guidelines—but not until after numerous schools had been stopped or discouraged by the board. Ironically, schools *joining* the 1000 School Challenge faced far greater administrative hurdles than the Dewson group had encountered launching it. They were victims of the visibility Dewson had created.

In January 2016, Dewson Street Public School welcomed a new family to its community. The organizing group had already exchanged messages with the Syrian family of five, but it was extraordinary to meet them for the first time. Once again, Dewson's population proved itself to be incredibly dedicated, competent and resourceful, helping the family to set up their home and navigate a new city, and checking in with them again and again. Principal Robinson recollected, "Schools Welcome Refugees galvanized students and the community. It set a tone of pride in what we'd achieved, and in our common goal. And it emphasized serving others, which is incredibly important."

Kelly is moved when she remembers an interaction between the Syrian mother and seven-year-old child her group sponsored. The duo was practising their English, and the mother tentatively read the word "community" aloud. "Oh, I know 'community'!" replied the boy. "It is like a family, we care for each other." Kelly is quite certain he learned that English word at his school, from the teachers and classmates who have made him feel welcome on a daily basis.

Parents have a valuable role to play in shaping schools, and it is the responsibility of any strong system to ensure that their voices are not merely heard, but given weight. When parents and schools work in partnership, goals can be translated into powerful action. These collaborations are vital to the effort of shaping our schools into institutions that will meet our children's needs and reflect the principles and skills we value. They also offer an important lesson in diplomacy and teamwork, showing kids how to be productive and engaged change-makers themselves.

EIGHT

IT'S ALL ABOUT
THE TEACHER

"The role of an individual teacher in a school is like a player on a football team or musician in an orchestra: all teachers are vital, but the culture of the school is even more important for the quality of the school."

—PASI SAHLBERG,
"Myth: You Can Do More With Less"[1]

When Kelly's daughter was in grade 4, her twelve-year-old friend came out as a girl—and Kelly was struck by her daughter's easy understanding and compassion. It turned out that, weeks earlier, her teacher had read a book to the class that opened up a conversation about gender, acceptance and support for differences. *X: A fabulous child's story* tells of a child spurned by adults because they can't tell if X is a girl or a boy. In the story, other children rally around and stand up for X. In class, the students had worked through the book's issues with their teacher. The experience was unremarkable to Kelly's daughter—she never mentioned it at home—but this "invisible" example of strong teaching was then used to real-world effect.

Every parent knows the difference an outstanding teacher makes. We see it in a child who begins to ask good questions about how the world works—or in one whose interest in school or self-esteem dramatically declines. Large-scale research clearly shows that in any given school year, the single biggest factor that affects how much a student will learn is his or her individual teacher.[2] It is no wonder that when we think of schools that meet students' changing needs, the first thing many think of is great educators.

The best teachers are active researchers, in two important ways. First, they are researchers of their students: they carefully observe their pupils, and from knowing them deeply, are able to engage them in learning that is both meaningful to their own lives and academically enriching. Second, they are researchers in the practice of teaching, actively seeking out strategies as educational data on the field evolves and children's needs change. We have seen these strengths in the work of teachers throughout this book: the team at George Webster who studied the possibilities of teaching math through a social justice lens; Lisa Lunney Borden who applied culturally specific strategies to the math curriculum; Rahim Essabhai who developed ways to ensure students had real-world problem-solving experience as part of the business program; Aaron Warner who facilitated his students' creativity through Genius Hour; Lianne McBride who determined her students' stressors and worked to relieve them.

All of these great teachers worked within a system that provided challenge and support for change. The George Webster team had committed to innovative approaches to teaching and learning through their Model Schools Program, which provided time and resources to develop cutting-edge improvements for students. Lunney Borden's innovative work around mathematics was a response to new Indigenous self-governing structures through Mi'kmaq Kina'matnewey (MK), and a recognition that the status quo was not good enough; MK did not just have goals, they built a relationship with the university to develop in-depth training for most teachers. Essabhai's interest in building community was charged into even greater action when his school connected him to the I-Think program and to leading researchers of applied creativity. Even Warner, experimenting in his own classroom with Genius Hour, gained confidence and concrete strategies through his professional learning network. When McBride was "stuck" with her students, it was her in-depth exposure to social-emotional learning practice through a province-wide initiative that gave her the tools and time to explore what worked in her classroom and to share her experience across her district.

All these success stories started with recognition of—and sometimes a push toward—the need to get better in order to meet high expectations for students. All of them involved various forms of support from a wider system that created an environment where taking risks is encouraged and where there is pressure to go beyond "good enough" or "comfortable."

Just as high expectations, pressure and support are important for students, they are important for teachers too. What lessons can we derive from the experiences of phenomenal teachers, and how can we integrate these into our system to support the work of all?

Defining High-Quality Teaching

Effective teachers have different styles—some may be more charismatic, while others may stand out for being supremely organized. Yet across these differences of styles, excellent teachers combine knowledge, skills and attitudes to help motivate students to push their own limits. In the United States, there has been considerable attention—even controversy—focused on defining effective or high-quality teaching. The Gates Foundation, for example, partnered with dozens of researchers and educational organizations to create the Measuring Effective Teaching (MET) project, which raised the suspicions of many teachers who feared it was a top-down effort to rank and control them. The project engaged over three thousand teachers—responsible for one hundred thousand students—in six school districts.[3] The efficacy of their teaching was measured through student surveys, classroom observations, video recordings, standardized test scores and value-added measures.[*]

Harvard University professor Dr. Ronald Ferguson was a key researcher in the project, and he and his company, Cambridge Education, worked with Ohio teachers to develop an assessment system for teacher performance. Together, they created a student survey designed to evaluate teachers' knowledge, pedagogy and relationships. The survey presents students with a series of statements designed to measure what they call the "7Cs" of good practice—challenge, control, care, confer, captivate, clarify and consolidate. For example: "Our teacher wants us to understand the material, not just memorize it" (*challenge*) or "My teacher seems to know if something is bothering me" (*confer*). The students respond to the statements with their level of agreement, on a scale from "Totally Untrue" to "Totally True."

This simple survey is a powerful measure of teacher quality, demonstrating strong alignment with trained observers' evaluations of teacher performance. It also suggests that the 7Cs map onto student performance in different ways. When students rated teachers highly on skills associated with academic press (challenge and control), on average they performed better on state-level standardized test scores. Support items (like care, confer, captivate, clarify and consolidate) were not closely linked to test-score achievement. Students in high-support classrooms, however, were much more likely to say that they were happy in

---

[*] Value-added measures use relatively complicated formulas to compare students' performance, usually on standardized tests, from the beginning of the year to the end of the year in order to try to isolate an individual teacher's contribution to learning.

school, and much more likely to be motivated to continue on to higher education. An over-emphasis on teacher performance tied to test scores alone misses these important contributors to social-emotional health and improved long-term outcomes for students, particularly those for whom college or university is not a presumed next step.

Ferguson is committed to examining the working and learning conditions that make great teaching possible. He has been able to show that institutional factors like facilities (can the students hear their teacher? do they have space to be active outside?) and resources (do teachers have good quality materials?) have a direct effect on teachers' commitment and performance, as do "teaching enablers" like responsive leadership, effective professional development and a strong school community. Ferguson's research shows that good and bad teachers do not exist in a vacuum—culture, context and resources matter.

Unions: Vehicles for Support and High Expectations

Teacher unions, although far from universally popular, have made significant contributions to improving the profession and schools. International research consistently shows that middle-class wages, positive working conditions and stable job opportunities are the strongest drivers of high-quality teaching[4]—and unions fight for all of these things. In addition, unions have contributed to a progressive change in the profession. The earliest unions in Ontario advocated for equal pay for women teachers, who, until well into the middle of the twentieth century, were paid half of what men were; Canadian unions were active in the early fight against LGBT discrimination, and fought against the automatic termination of teachers who became pregnant. And in an ongoing way, unions provide an important support for teachers against potential or actual abuses of power by their employers.

In public perception, however, the advantages of unions are often overshadowed by the protection they offer "bad" teachers. A *Maclean's* article titled "Why It's So Hard to Fire Bad Teachers" states:

> According to Barrie Bennett, a professor at the Ontario Institute for Studies in Education, the dismissal process is so onerous, the risk of reprisal from teachers' unions so great, that "most principals find it's not worth the effort." Instead, they approve transfers, or hide struggling teachers where their deficiencies can go unnoticed. The result however, is this: a system that keeps incompetent teachers in the classroom.[5]

In most provinces, it *is* difficult to fire teachers. Unions are protective of educators and typically require significant proof of misconduct if they are to take action. The idea that job security is a bad thing, however, is a red herring. Having a secure work environment with adequate working conditions is helpful to the development of the profession. High turnover isn't good for school quality, and the threat of being fired actually works against the kind of creative risk-taking we need. Moreover, firing bad teachers might seem like a silver bullet to fix schools (or at least, provide catharsis), but it is not in fact a particularly promising way to make schools better. We are unaware of any major effort to rate the quality of teachers in Canada, but the MET project estimates that 6 percent of U.S. teachers perform their jobs poorly. It is not unreasonable to think that the percentage in Canada is similar (or perhaps even lower, since Canadian teachers, on average, are more qualified*). A strategy based on firing teachers

---

* Here, teachers are required to have a Bachelor of Education degree and in-school experience.

addresses only six percent of the teacher workforce and appears indifferent to what is happening in most classrooms. In fact, research shows that parents view their child's school and teacher more favourably than they view the system as a whole. A recent survey of public attitudes toward education in Ontario revealed that only 52 percent of the public would assign the province's schools an A or B grade; but when parents were specifically asked to grade their child's school, 81 percent of them awarded it an A or B grade.[6] Similarly, 69 percent of Ontarians are very or somewhat satisfied with the job teachers are doing generally, but 77 percent are very or somewhat satisfied with their child's teacher.

The Alberta Teachers' Association (ATA) offers a notable example of how a union can advocate effectively for its members while promoting high standards within the profession. Over the past twenty years, the ATA has done a remarkable job of vigorously representing the interests of its members while actively courting the support of parents and the public. The ATA has legislative responsibility—and is publicly perceived—as a key defender of professional standards.

Union detractors may be surprised to learn that much of ATA's success appears to flow from its exceptionally broad powers: atypically, it represents both teachers *and* school leaders, and it represents teachers while holding responsibility for professional regulation (in the same way that doctors and lawyers have responsibility for certification and discipline).* By contrast,

---

* The association, in fact, chooses not to call itself a union, because, according to its executive secretary, Gordon Thomas, "the label makes a difference. . . . We tend not to say 'union,' because of the nature of our organization, which combines union and professional responsibilities."

in Ontario, principals are not represented by a union, and self-regulation of both teachers and principals (including licensing and discipline) is handled by a statutory body, the Ontario College of Teachers. In the 1990s, when the Progressive Conservative government of Mike Harris removed principals from the province's teacher union it undermined cohesive organizational cultures by reinforcing labour-management relationships rather than collegial ones *within* schools. By establishing the Ontario College of Teachers, the government further fractured educators' ability to speak with one voice through their unions. On the other hand, the College was seen as putting teachers on an equal footing with other self-regulated professions, like doctors and lawyers. There are, however, significant differences between these professions, since the vast majority of teachers in the province are public employees with job security, not self-employed workers with control over the terms and conditions of their work and some vulnerability to market pressure.

Although it may seem preferable to have multiple institutions speaking for teachers, the ATA is able to address problems with a level of efficiency and consistency that is rare nationwide. ATA executive secretary Gordon Thomas believes that there are significant advantages to having a single association: "Because we don't only represent our members, we have substantial responsibilities in public interest—and these are good things that get headlines," he explained, "Those headlines tend to be helpful in making the case that what's best for kids is often best for teachers. It is easier to make some of those arguments because [our work is] more than self-interest."

In its union functions, the ATA has been exceptionally effective—certainly assisted by Alberta's relative economic prosperity for the last twenty years.* The association has settled three long-term collective agreements in a row since 2002. In 2006, teachers committed to five years of labour peace for a deal that involved the government taking over one third, or $2.1 billion, of their unfunded pension liability. They also negotiated for wage increases on the same accelerator as those received by members of the Legislative Assembly, which are higher than cost-of-living raises. Then in 2013, they settled a four-year contract with limited wage increases but important workload concessions, with the government promising to conduct an internal review and a third-party study to examine how teacher workloads could be amended.

Remarkably, the ATA has negotiated these agreements without striking, employing work-to-rule or withdrawing extracurricular activities. The province has conservative labour laws in place that would treat work-to-rule as an illegal strike, but the ATA's tactics are also highly strategic. According to Thomas, "In Alberta, you just wouldn't see work-to-rule. Our history is we go on strike, we don't mess around with half measures. You either do all the job, or none of it. In doing so you build a well of support."

Work-to-rule wears down both the professional image of teachers and support from the public. Although the point of work-to-rule is to highlight just how much educators do, when teachers withdraw from non-contractually required activities, like providing report card comments and supporting extracurricular activities, the strategy implies the narrowest conception of education

---

* The year 2015–2016 saw dramatic changes in Alberta politics, with the election of a new NDP government as well as a sudden drop in oil prices that has created unprecedented fiscal pressures. It will be interesting to monitor how the ATA will work both with this new government (which is more closely aligned with their politics than the former Progressive Conservative government) and in a more economically challenging environment.

and reduces the job of the teacher to the isolated work of the classroom. In Ontario—despite years of a relatively teacher-friendly provincial government—there has been a heavy reliance on work-to-rule as a bargaining tactic, and it is extremely unpopular with the public. Only 44 percent of Ontarians polled during the last round of bargaining supported the teachers (although even fewer supported the government). A significant majority disapproved of work-to-rule tactics: 62 percent opposed the withdrawal of extracurriculars, and 71 percent disapproved of teachers not writing comments on report cards.[7] And because work-to-rule is a "half measure," and not a full strike, the message implicitly communicated to the public is that the stakes are not *that* high for teachers. Even when bargaining is over a significant issue that would be likely to garner public support, like reducing kindergarten class sizes to fewer than thirty students in the 2015 round of negotiations, the message often is not heard.

The last time the ATA went on strike, back in 2002, it prioritized connecting with parents and the public, via pamphleting and media outreach, to build support for teachers and the issues they confronted in the classrooms. By the time its members convened for the strike vote, the ATA's internal polling showed that the percentage of parents who thought that classroom funding was too low had risen, in four years, from 36 to 72 percent. (By contrast, in the 2014 B.C. teachers' strike, the majority of the public felt that neither unions nor the government had demonstrated that they cared about the best interests of children.[8]) Successful mobilization and ongoing popularity have had lasting impacts on the ATA's bargaining power.

The other key contributor to the ATA's popularity with the public has been its role as a guardian of professional standards. As mentioned earlier, the ATA is unique in Canada in that it prosecutes professional misconduct (a responsibility handled elsewhere by the provincial government or a separate college of teachers)—and it does so with relative alacrity and severity.

In March 2016, for example, the ATA received a number of complaints about the conduct of Louis-Georges Pelletier, a French Immersion high school teacher in Red Deer, Alberta. Although complaints about Pelletier had been made to the school board for many years (these had been settled individually with monitoring and remediation plans), when they were finally referred to the ATA, quick action followed. By April, the ATA was conducting a disciplinary hearing.

At the hearing, in a statement of facts, the incidents highlighted by thirty students and seven staff members included Pelletier ridiculing a student who had made an error on a test by loudly asking her if she were dyslexic, and forcing a shorter student to stand on a desk to speak, claiming that otherwise he could not hear him. He told a child who had missed class to go to her grandmother's funeral that school was more important than family. He made homophobic remarks, described another teacher as being "of the wrong colour" and expressed the view that women should stay at home and tend to babies. Six of the students said they had left French Immersion to avoid Pelletier. Several reported that his conduct had caused not only mortification but anxiety and depression, and one boy said Pelletier's homophobia had been a contributing factor in his suicide attempt, which had resulted in hospitalization.

At the hearing, Pelletier pleaded guilty to two counts of professional misconduct: for failing to treat students with respect and dignity, and for failing to uphold the honour of the profession. The Professional Conduct Committee suspended him from the profession for six months—thus ensuring he could not teach in the public, French or Catholic systems in the province—and issued a letter of serious reprimand. He resigned during the hearing after admitting he humiliated and bullied students in an agreed statement of facts.[9] Over a ten-year period, the ATA has conducted 728 investigations and 138 hearings, and ordered 23 suspensions and 25 expulsions.[10] The school board chair, Bev Manning, has been quoted in the Red Deer paper praising the ATA for the work it does "to ensure its profession is accountable to students and the community."[11]

Thomas also points to other factors that have boosted the professional reputation and functionality of the ATA. It has a tradition of generating its own carefully researched policy options and ensuring its members can speak authoritatively about the experiences of teachers across the province. And it has a substantial, province-wide structure for professional development and representation. Alongside local workshops bolstering relevant skills and competencies, the ATA convenes high-profile provincial events.* Finally, because teachers and principals are represented by the same union, Thomas argues that their working relationship is strengthened, defined by collegiality instead of by hostility between staff and management. Thomas argues that "conversations are not about who does what, if or when it should be done, but how best to meet student learning needs." Certainly, collegial environments exist in schools where principals are not union members, but it is striking that there were only fifteen arbitrations in Alberta in 2015.

When it comes to making schools work well for children, Thomas believes that "government doesn't have all the answers, and should rely on the profession to help them figure it out." No

---

* In one example, the ATA held a conference on "growing up digital in Alberta" to analyze what the use of technology means for kids and society—an event born of a research co-operation between the union and Harvard University to better understand the health impacts of technology use.

one would think of redesigning the health care system without doctors and their representative organizations. Bringing teachers' voices to the process of running the enterprise of public education has always been at the forefront of the ATA's action and agenda. Larry Booi, the former ATA president, recalls his early engagement in the union as a social studies teacher in a Catholic school in southern Alberta: "Part of the frustration I felt as a young teacher was that a lot of the issues that had an impact on the work I did with kids were outside of my control. If I had thirty-eight kids in my class, that was caused by administrative or political decisions. Some of your effort has to go to the big picture, trying to nudge the supertanker."

The ATA has developed a range of ways to ensure teachers' voices are heard, from representation on all provincial curriculum committees to striking a blue-ribbon panel on inclusive education to working to shift the province's approach to accountability. One of their victories has been shaping province-wide testing to better meet teachers' needs. Like all North American teacher unions, the ATA is opposed to province-wide testing (except at graduation) on the basis that it generates a very narrow slice of information often used to stigmatize schools and teachers—particularly those working with students who are facing greater challenges. Thomas remembers one of his colleagues ridiculously, and harmfully, being labelled "the worst teacher in Alberta" based on twenty-five multiple-choice questions answered by her twenty-three grade 3 students. The ATA was successful in shifting province-wide testing to the beginning of the year, so that teachers can use it as a diagnostic evaluation tool—rather than at the end of the year, when it is too late to propel any action.

The association has had other policy wins too. When the Alberta government began making adjustments to the math curriculum to accommodate parents' demand for more "basics," the ATA succeeded in ensuring students would retain the space to study subjects in depth and in applied ways. And when the government proposed spending sixty-six million dollars a year on merit pay for teachers whose test scores went up, the ATA countered with the evidence that merit pay is ineffective in producing school improvement, and suggested an alternative approach that would use those funds for professional learning; under the Alberta Initiative for School Improvement (AISI), teachers could apply for grants to develop local initiatives that they believed would improve their schools and foster community connections.

The ATA is remarkable because it is a union in which teachers are actively shaping not just wages and working conditions but the broader system of education. It appears to have struck a balance among vociferously advocating for its members on economic and workplace issues, maintaining a standard of professional excellence through discipline and building public support for the profession. This balancing act is not simple, but it is surely instructive in thinking about how unions can help be positive contributors to schools of the future.

Great Systems Develop Great Teachers

The systems that envelop educators, and to which unions respond, can enable or deter great teaching. There are over 630,000 teachers and early childhood educators in Canada's public schools, and many are not receiving the supports necessary to take their teaching to the next level. Although teachers' salaries are the single biggest expense of our education system, making up 63 percent of education budgets nationally (and a similar share of education budgets internationally[12]), many teachers still feel underpaid and undervalued, a sentiment that can bleed into their work. Other countries with high-performing students and comparatively supportive systems provide an interesting set of comparisons and valuable lessons for Canada.

Finland and Singapore have moved from high-dropout, low-achievement profiles to the very top of international student rankings in math, science and literacy within little more than a generation. And both countries have had successful national economic turnarounds driven by education. Finland has transitioned from a rural, resource-driven economy to one characterized by high technology and high employment, and Singapore has shifted from an impoverished outpost into a wealthy, export-driven city-state. In 2015, on the Programme for International Student Assessment (PISA), Singapore ranked first globally in science, math, and reading; 39 percent of Singaporean students were considered "high performing" in at least one subject, compared to an international average of 15 percent. Singapore's reading performance is especially impressive, since almost half of its students do not speak English at home. Finland was fifth in science, and ranked fourth in reading and twelfth in math, with a notably small achievement gap between its richest and poorest students.[13] Both systems boast very high rates of secondary school completion—almost 95 percent, compared to Canada's 85 percent.[14*] Canada's PISA results were also impressive, with the ranking of fourth among countries overall. While we continued to decline in math, we were seventh in science, second in reading, and tenth in math. Although a consistent high performer, Canada hasn't had the same "turnaround narrative" that the other two countries have enjoyed.

---

* Note that there is significant variation among the provinces' and territories' secondary school completion rate. Only 35 percent of students in Nunavut graduate from high school, and only 69 percent in Alberta.

Like Canada, Finland and Singapore are both relatively wealthy countries. Both have strong social welfare nets, and both have high public school enrolment. In fact, there are no private schools in Singapore for the first six years of formal education, and the private high school sector is considered inferior to the best public schools—a way of paying your way around meritocracy. But the overt similarities end there. Unlike Canada, both Finland and Singapore have elevated education to a priority of the highest national importance. In Singapore, education funding comes second only to defence spending in the public budget;[15] in Finland, it is second only to health, by a relatively small margin (education receives 88 percent of what health does).[16] In Canada, expenditures on education as a percentage of GDP are less than half those devoted to health.[17*]

Notably, national polls suggest that teaching is one of the most desirable and respected professions in both Singapore and Finland, behind medicine but ahead of almost all others. Admission to the profession is highly competitive. In Finland, teachers are required to have a research-based master's degree. Students admitted to Singapore's teaching institution are paid a stipend to attend. While high academic performance is a prerequisite, both systems require significant evidence of commitment and suitability that go well beyond grades.

Across both countries' systems, the emphases on retaining teachers and teacher learning are central to the policy framework. In Singapore, the level of attrition from the teaching profession is very low—only 2.4 percent—and teachers receive significant

---

* According to the OECD, between 2011 and 2015 Canada spent 5.3 percent of GDP on education. The Canadian Institute of Health Information reports Canada spent 10.9 percent of GDP on health care in 2015 and suggests 10 percent of GDP was spent on health care in 2014.

bonuses for staying in the workforce. Professional development has been made a priority. Singaporean teachers receive paid professional education time roughly equivalent to that of Canadian educators (approximately one hundred hours), and they are *also* given "professional development periods" in their weekly timetables. Pathways have been developed to raise expectations of teachers and encourage them to advance through the profession: "master teachers" are selected by their peers, and have defined roles within their schools as mentors and coaches. Teachers who are recognized as outstanding are also rewarded by opportunities for further learning, through paid sabbaticals and scholarships for local and overseas study. In Canada (as in most countries), the only path to advancement is by becoming an administrator, meaning great teachers have to leave the classroom.

Both Finland and Singapore have explicitly emphasized the connection between schooling and the economic and social goals for their societies as a whole. Both countries are more than a decade into educational programs based on broad, holistic curricular goals. Since 2004, Finland has had a mandatory focus on arts and crafts, alongside personal development linked with citizenship. Singapore developed the Thinking Schools, Learning Nation program in 1997, and in 2004 its emphasis shifted from knowledge to skills and attitudes—specifically, creativity, critical thinking and "concerned citizens/active contributors." Singapore's new emphasis sits uncomfortably with its strict system of high-stakes examinations at different stages, influential school rankings and relatively little room for dissent—but schools increasingly try to distinguish themselves in these areas. When they broadened their focuses from traditional emphases to applied, creative and social-emotional learning, both countries' test scores rose.

There are differences between Finland and Singapore in both context and policy. Finland is an example of classic,

Scandinavian-model collaborative governance, with a demographically homogeneous, officially bilingual, population; Singapore is far more authoritarian, and ethnically, religiously and linguistically diverse. Finland has a strongly unionized teacher workforce (more than 95 percent of educators are members), whereas Singapore's union represents only about half of teachers and lacks collective bargaining rights. Finland does not have any formal system of teacher evaluation, while Singapore has an extensive assessment system. Since 2005, Singapore's teachers have been graded annually on how they have achieved performance objectives, using a mix of peer observations and teaching and student portfolios. Furthermore, Singapore uses a merit pay scale with increases that range from 10 to 30 percent, whereas Finland has a pay scale its most public advocate describes as "exceptionally flat."[18] Singapore has a full system of exam-based national assessment starting in grade 4; in Finland, there is only one national assessment, which comes at the end of secondary school. Almost all Singaporean leaders of government and business have attended a small handful of "top" schools, whereas in Finland, most students attend their local schools, which generally perform equivalently. Finland's class sizes are small; Singapore's are large.[19] In Singapore, there is widespread use of private tutoring, while in Finland, there is a public commitment to providing all children with access to free or low-cost recreation and arts programs.

Finnish teachers work far fewer hours per week than their counterparts in Singapore or Canada—perhaps partly as a result of smaller class sizes, but also perhaps because of differences in work cultures. According to an international study based on time diaries, on average Finnish junior secondary teachers work thirty-six hours per week, as opposed to fifty-six in Singapore and fifty-eight in Alberta. In Singapore, as in most of North America, teachers work many unpaid hours beyond those prescribed in their contracts. In Singapore, only about a third of working time is spent in front of the classroom, compared to 60 percent in Finland and 45 percent in Alberta.[20]

These differences suggest that there is more than one right way to arrive at a strong policy framework for teachers. Not all of Finland's and Singapore's policies would work well in Canada—the working hours of Finnish teachers, for example, would likely be unattainable—but our country could nonetheless learn from some of what these education systems do best. Teachers in Singapore and Finland are highly regarded, allowing for selectivity in recruitment, and are supported by active professional development. Canada is relatively selective; more people want to pursue a teaching career than are accepted into teaching programs, and in most parts of Canada actually getting a teaching job is highly competitive. Professional development is provided, but varies widely across the country and even within provinces. There is little policy attention paid to coherence or effectiveness of professional development. There are very limited opportunities for teachers to advance within the field. Teachers typically feel underappreciated—and in our view, they are. Respect for teachers could use a boost. The other key takeaway from these successful systems is that their teachers and schools are not doing it alone. In both countries, children are the recipients of extensive out-of-school learning opportunities, social safety nets limit inequality, and above all, education is a top priority in a way that saturates society at large. In Canada, this is much more hit and miss, and too often dependent on extraordinary efforts in individual schools.

Final Thoughts
This is the ultimate challenge in education: how do we take the good work that is evident in pockets of schools and slices of the

system and spread it widely? What needs to happen so that every teacher and every school can push the limits of what is possible?

Looking at the success of systems like Finland, Singapore and, more locally, Mi'kmaw Kina'matnewey, we can see some common themes. In all of these places, students' learning doesn't stop when they exit the building; education and educators are highly valued, and are seen as the key to a better, more equitable future; teacher development is identified as a critical piece of the puzzle; and teachers are given time and resources to improve their practice collaboratively. Instead of a "gotcha" culture, in which the public is positioned outside the system and ready to blame or demonize it, schools are seen as community institutions that live within a broader network of social institutions. Schools are rooted in their communities, and communities are rooted in their schools.

Moving forward, we must challenge every level of the education system to continue to learn. We need a culture of pushing the limits, that focuses less on pointing the finger and more on working together until every child is succeeding—one in which both teachers and students are made to feel supported and secure, and encouraged to surpass expectations. Every class is different. Every student is different. Every school is different. And yet, there is a body of knowledge about what works in education. Educators need to be given time and support to learn from each other, and from this research, the opportunity to identify what is working and challenge themselves and each other to change what is not.

Dialogue about the best way to reform education is usually framed around diametrically opposed views. The math wars are a great example: pressure vacillates between more focus on the basics and more focus on problem-solving. In math, as in the system at large, the solution lies somewhere in the middle, integrating the best of both approaches. The best schools support students' basic knowledge needs while providing enriched, demanding academic programs. They pay attention to their social-emotional needs without sacrificing the cognitive challenges that will make them successful—and vice versa. The best systems find a balance between supporting their teachers and demanding that they continuously improve their practice. They push their students, their educators and their communities to learn deeply, ask complicated questions and pursue complex answers. The best schools challenge the status quo. This is the work we need to engage in as a collective if our students are to be the successful, engaged citizens our world requires.

To give children the education they need, we are arguing for leadership, learning and pressure at every level: student, staff, principal, parent, community, school board and government. Everyone must be a partner. Maintaining high expectations is essential, and if it is to be more than rhetoric it requires sustained effort and a willingness to change age-old structures. One of the few certainties in our unknown future is that students will need the ability to solve problems, be strong people and actively participate in a wider community to thrive. In working together, we can expand our conception of what is possible today and tomorrow, and prepare them for that future.

ACKNOWLEDGEMENTS

So many people have played a role in bringing this project to fruition. Many thanks to all the educators, parents, students and researchers we interviewed. You were generous with your time and insights, and contributed to both the final book and all the learning behind it. You inspire us!

Thank you to Sakaana Yasotharan; Saida Mohamed; Ayan Bade; Aiman Flahat; Rahim Essabhai; Colin Walmsley; Bernard Soubry; Caroline Leps; Devin Grant; Benjamin Mappin-Kasirer; Bogdan Knezevic; Brittany Graham; Alexa Yakubovitch; Logan Graham; Ingrid Palmer and her children; Rosalie Bernardo; Kim Pividor; Steve Corke; Rehanna Ayube; Dale Morris; Robin Coyle; Dianne Balkos; Dimitra Tsolos; Ken Dewey; Debbie Grounds; Jason James; Terry Doyle; Aqilah Goraya; Dionne Warwick; Mohammed and his family; Rolando Carrillo; Jimmy Madeira; Leena Augimeri; Nicola Slater; Paul Henry; Bobby Crane; Lisa Lunney Borden; Wendy Mackey; Tiannie Paul; Aaron Prosper; John Jerome Paul; Susan Hopkins; Stuart Shanker; Alan Dunfield; Truly Urquart; Bob Eckstein; Annie Kidder; David Cameron; Megan Yeadon; Helen Fisher; Robert S. Brown; Rosalie Bender; Sheila Cary-Meagher; Vidya Shah; Beverly Caswell; Indigo Esmonde; Joe Flessa; Carol Campbell; Nina Bascia; Aaron Warner and his students Chloe, Isaac and Abby; Jon Nichols; Ellen Spencer; Roger Martin; Nogah Kornberg; Lianne McBride; Taunya Shaw; Shelley Hymel; Lisa Pedrini; Mike McKay; Roger Weissberg; Carl Corter; Heather Highet; Mike Smith; Hayley AvRuskin; Varinia Vartolas; Corvin Cioata; Tom Chau; Michael Chechile; Kim Meldrum; Susan Connery; Nathalie Charland; Becca Ainsley; Anne Jenkins; Joseph Kahne; David Stocker; Tessa Hill; Lia Valente; Larry Cuban; Lina Cino; Rob MacKinnon; John Au; Jacqui Strachan; David Johnson; Paule Langevin; Don Barclay; Eid Ismaili and his son; Jeff Crane; Janice Robinson; Dewson School Community Refugees Welcome and the Dewson School Council, especially D. Williams, Sarah Spencer, Tori Smith and Maryjean Lancefield; Suzy Dabaghian; Bedros Guleserian; Jennifer Brodie and Kathryn Richards; Larry Booi; Gordon Thomas; Denise Belchetz; Bill Hogarth; Lyn Sharratt; Jackie Young; Ruth Hall; Ruth Baumann; Charles Ungerleider and Charles Pascal.

A special thank-you goes out to all of the teachers at George Webster Elementary School, Superintendents Vicky Branco and Roula Anastasakos, researcher Maria Yau and other members of the Toronto District School Board who allowed us to draw from Nancy's experiences working there as an educator. We have both also learned a great deal as advocates and parents in the TDSB community. Kelly is very grateful to the two outstanding educational research institutions where she has studied schooling with an eye on change: the Ontario Institute for Studies in Education of the University of Toronto and People for Education. Many of the principals whose stories we shared are Nancy's colleagues in the Canada's Outstanding Principals Network. We thank the Learning Partnership for creating and supporting this network.

This book would not exist without the vision, passion, skill and patience of our incredibly talented editor, Martha Kanya-Forstner. Your belief that we as a society need to learn from the front lines of education was the reason that we—neither of us professional writers—had the chance to write this book. It has been an incredible learning experience, and we are grateful for it, and to both Martha and Melanie Tutino for their craft in producing a much-refined final manuscript. Another big thank-you to everyone else at Penguin Random House Canada who shepherded us through this process: Amy Black, Trish Bunnett, Five Seventeen, Tara Tovell and Emily Wilson.

Finally, neither one of us could have completed this book without tremendous personal support: for wise and sustaining conversations, thanks to Rosemary, Geoff, Jeannie and Joanna. To our families, above all—Sammy, Sam, Xin and Nuan—our thanks for sharing us with this book.

ENDNOTES

CHAPTER ONE: BEYOND THE BASICS

1   Royal Commission on Education in Ontario, *Report of the Royal Commission on Education in Ontario* (Toronto: Queen's Printer, 1950), 31.

2   Organisation for Economic Co-operation and Development, *Pisa 2015: Results in Focus* (Paris: OECD Publishing, 2016), 5, http://www.oecd.org/pisa/pisa-2015-results-in-focus.pdf; Organisation for Economic Co-operation and Development, *PISA 2012 Results: What Students Know and Can Do; Student Performance in Mathematics, Reading and Science (Volume I)* (Paris: OECD Publishing, 2014), 19, accessed from http://www.oecd.org/pisa/keyfindings/pisa-2012-results-volume-1.htm.

3   Caroline Alphonso, "Canada's Fall in Math-Education Ranking Sets Off Alarm Bells," *The Globe and Mail*, December 3, 2013, http://www.theglobeandmail.com/news/national/education/canadas-fall-in-math-education-ranking-sets-off-red-flags/article15730663.

4   David Staples, Great Canadian Math Debate (forty-four part series), *Edmonton Journal*, 2014.

5   *Cross Country Checkup with Duncan McCue*, "Is There Something Wrong with the Way Math is Being Taught?," radio broadcast recording, CBC Radio, published May 31, 2015, http://www.cbc.ca/radio/checkup/is-there-something-wrong-with-the-way-math-is-being-taught-1.3093910.

6   Anna Stokke, "What to Do about Canada's Declining Math Scores," *C.D. Howe Institute Commentary*, no. 427 (May 2015): 8, https://www.cdhowe.org/sites/default/files/attachments/research_papers/mixed/commentary_427.pdf.

7   Organisation for Economic Co-operation and Development, *PISA 2012 Results: What Students Know and Can Do; Student Performance in Mathematics, Reading and Science*, 61.

8   Hanover Research, "Bringing 21st Century Skill Development to the
     Forefront of K–12 Education," *Hanover Blog*, September 24, 2014,
     http://www.hanoverresearch.com/2014/09/24/bringing-21st-century-skill-
     development-to-the-forefront-of-k-12-education.

9   "Employability Skills 2000+," Conference Board of Canada, accessed March 10,
     2017, http://www.conferenceboard.ca/topics/education/learning-tools/employ-
     ability-skills.aspx.

10   Canadian Council of Chief Executives, *Preliminary Survey Report: The Skill
     Needs of Major Canadian Employers* (Ottawa: Canadian Council of Chief
     Executives, 2014), http://www.ceocouncil.ca/wp-content/uploads/2014/01/
     Preliminary-report-on-skills-survey-Jan-20-2014-2.pdf; Aon Hewitt and
     Business Council of Canada, *Developing Canada's Future Workforce: A Survey
     of Large Private-Sector Employers* (Ottawa, 2016), http://thebusinesscouncil.ca/
     wp-content/uploads/2016/03/Developing-Canadas-Future-Workforce.pdf.

11   Ontario Non-Profit Housing Association, *Waiting Lists Survey 2010: ONPHA's
     2010 Report on Waiting List Statistics for Ontario* (Toronto: Ontario Non-Profit
     Housing Association, 2010), 4.

12   Model Schools for Inner City Task Force, *Model Schools for Inner City Task
     Force Report* (Toronto: Toronto District School Board, 2005).

13   William G. Huit, "Bloom et al.'s Taxonomy of the Cognitive Domain,"
     Educational Psychology Interactive, published 2011, http://www.edpsycinter-
     active.org/topics/cognition/bloom.html.

14   Harold Wenglinsky, "Closing the Racial Achievement Gap: The Roles of
     Reforming Instructional Practices," *Education Policy Analysis* 12, no. 64
     (November 2004), accessed December 2, 2004, from the Education Policy
     Analysis Archives, http://dx.doi.org/10.14507/epaa.v12n64.2004; Fred M.
     Newmann, Anthony S. Bryk, and Jenny K. Nagaoka, *Authentic Intellectual
     Work and Standardized Tests: Conflict or Coexistence?* (Chicago: Chicago
     Consortium on School Reform, 2001), https://consortium.uchicago.edu/sites/
     default/files/publications/p0a02.pdf.

15   Anna Stokke, "Too Much Math Education Is Based on Pet Theories," *The
     Globe and Mail*, September 8, 2014, http://www.theglobeandmail.com/news/
     national/education/too-much-math-education-is-based-on-pet-theories/
     article20369587.

16   Louis Alfieri et al., "Does Discovery-Based Instruction Enhance Learning?,"
     Journal of Educational Psychology 103, no. 1 (February 2011): 1–18.

17   National Mathematics Advisory Panel, *Foundations for Success: The Final
     Report of the National Mathematics Advisory Panel* (Washington, D.C.: U.S.
     Department of Education, 2008), xiv.

18   James. E. Ridgeway, et al., "Student Attainment in the Connected
     Mathematics Curriculum," in *Standards-Based School Mathematics Curricula:
     What Are They? What Do Students Learn?*, ed. Sharon L. Senk and Denisse R.
     Thompson (Mahwah, N.J.: Lawrence Erlbaum Associates, 2003), 193–224;

Julie E. Riordan and Pendred E. Noyce, "The Impact of Two Standards-Based Mathematics Curricula on Student Achievement in Massachusetts," *Journal for Research in Mathematics Education* 32, no. 4 (July 2001): 368–398; Alan H. Schoenfeld, "Making Mathematics Work for All Children: Issues of Standards, Testing, and Equity," *Educational Researcher* 31, no. 1 (January/February 2002): 13–25; Alan H. Schoenfeld, "Mathematics Education in the Twentieth Century," in *Education Across a Century: The Centennial Volume*, ed. Lyn Corno (Chicago: National Society for the Study of Education, 2001), 239–278.

19   National Mathematics Advisory Panel, *Foundations for Success: The Final Report of the National Mathematics Advisory Panel.*

20   National Research Council (U.S.) et al., *Successful K–12 STEM Education: Identifying Effective Approaches* (Washington, D.C.: The National Academies Press, 2011).

21   Lisa Delpit, *"Multiplication Is for White People": Raising Expectations for Other People's Children* (New York: The New Press, 2012).

22   Robert Rosenthal and Lenore Jacobson, *Pygmalion in the Classroom: Teacher Expectation and Pupils' Intellectual Development* (New York: Holt, Reinhart and Winston, 1968).

23   Christine M. Rubie-Davies, John Hattie and Richard Hamilton, "Expecting the Best for Students: Teacher Expectations and Academic Outcomes," *British Journal of Educational Psychology* 76, part 3 (2006): 429–444; Education Commission of the States, *Progress of Education Reform December 2012, Vol. 13, No. 6: Teacher Expectations of Students: A Self-Fulfilling Prophecy* (Denver, Education Commission of the States, 2012).

24   William Jeynes, "A Meta-analysis: The Effects of Parental Involvement on Minority Children's Academic Achievement," *Education and Urban Society* 35, no. 2 (February 2003): 202–218; William Jeynes, "A Meta-analysis of the Relation of Parental Involvement to Urban Elementary School Student Academic Achievement," *Urban Education* 40, no. 3 (May 2005): 237–269; William Jeynes, "The Relationship Between Parental Involvement and Urban Secondary School Student Academic Achievement: A Meta-analysis," *Urban Education* 42, no. 1 (January 2007): 82–110.

25   Valerie E. Lee and Julia B. Smith, "Social Support and Achievement for Young Adolescents in Chicago: The Role of School Academic Press," *American Educational Research Journal* 36, no. 4 (Winter 1999): 907–945; National Research Council (U.S.) et al., *Achieving High Educational Standards for All: Conference Summary* (Washington, D.C.: National Academies Press, 2002); National Research Council (U.S.) et al., *Engaging Schools: Fostering High School Students' Motivation to Learn* (Washington, D.C.: National Academies Press, 2004).

26   "Mi'kimaqs Recall Hunger at Residential School," *CBC News*, July 18, 2013, http://www.cbc.ca/news/canada/nova-scotia/mi-kmaqs-recall-hunger-at-residential-school-1.1337440.

27 Ontario Ministry of Education, *Paying Attention to Spatial Reasoning, K–12* (Ottawa: Queen's Printer for Ontario, 2014), 3.

28 "Mawkinumasultinej! Let's Learn Together! Quill Work," Show Me Your Math, accessed July 31, 2016, http://showmeyourmath.ca/?page_id=85.

29 *The Canadian Encyclopedia Online*, s.v. "Mi'kmaq," accessed December 23, 2015, http://www.thecanadianencyclopedia.ca/en/article/micmac-mikmaq.

30 Mi'kmaw Kina'matnewey, *Annual Report 2015–16* (Membertou, N.S.: Mi'kmaw Kina'matnewey, 2016), 163, http://kinu.ca/sites/default/files/doc /2014/Feb/mk_2016_annual_report_draft_.pdf.

31 "2011 June Status Report of the Auditor General of Canada to the House of Commons: Chapter 4; Programs for First Nations on Reserves," Office of the Auditor General of Canada, June 2011, http://www.oag-bvg.gc.ca/internet/ English/parl_oag_201106_04_e_35372.html#hd5e; Nova Scotia Department of Education and Early Childhood Development, *Accountability Report 2014–15* (Halifax: Nova Scotia Department of Education and Early Childhood Development, 2015), 19, http://novascotia.ca/government/accountability/ 2015-2016/2015-2016-EECD-Accountability-Report.pdf.

CHAPTER TWO: TEACHING CREATIVITY

1 Jeffrey K. Smith and Lisa F. Smith, "Educational Creativity," in *The Cambridge Handbook of Creativity*, eds. James C. Kaufman & Robert J. Sternberg (Cambridge: Cambridge University Press, 2010), 251.

2 Ken Robinson, "TED Talk: Do Schools Kill Creativity?," TED video, (February 2006), https://www.ted.com/talks/ken_robinson_says_schools_kill_ creativity?language=en.

3 National Advisory Committee on Creative and Cultural Education, *All Our Futures: Creativity, Culture and Education; Report to the Secretary of State for Education and Employment [and] the Secretary of State for Culture, Media & Sport* (London: Department for Education and Employment, 1999), http://sirkenrobinson.com/pdf/allourfutures.pdf.

4 Ronald A. Beghetto and J.C. Kaufman, *Nurturing Creativity in the Classroom* (Cambridge and New York: Cambridge University Press, 2010).

5 Bill Lucas, Guy Claxton and Ellen Spencer, *Progression in Student Creativity in School: First Steps Towards New Forms of Formative Assessments*, OECD Working Paper No.86 (Paris: OECD Publishing, 2014), 14.

6 Josh Wingrove, "Toronto's New Murder Capital," *The Globe and Mail*, July 17, 2009, http://www.theglobeandmail.com/news/toronto/torontos-new-murder- capital/article4327089/?page=all.

7 Ken Robinson, "TED Talk: Do Schools Kill Creativity?"

CHAPTER THREE: SOCIAL-EMOTIONAL LEARNING

1   Interview with Kelly Gallagher-Mackay, August 2015.

2   "Core SEL Competencies," Collaborative for Academic, Social, and
     Emotional Learning, http://www.casel.org/core-competencies.

3   "Employability Skills 2000+," Conference Board of Canada; Canadian Council
     of Chief Executives, *Preliminary Survey Report: The Skill Needs of Major
     Canadian Employers*; Aon Hewitt and Business Council of Canada, *Developing
     Canada's Future Workforce: A Survey of Large Private-Sector Employers*.

4   Samuel Bowles and Herbert Gintis, *Schooling in Capitalist America:
     Educational Reform and the Contradictions of Economic Life* (London:
     Routledge and Keegan Paul, 1976).

5   James Heckman, Jora Stixrud and Sergio Urzua, "The Effects of Cognitive
     and Noncognitive Abilities on Labour Market Outcomes and Social
     Behaviour," *Journal of Labor Economics* 24, no. 3 (July 2006): 411–484; James
     Heckman and Yona Rubenstein, "The Importance of Noncognitive Skills:
     Lessons from the GED Testing Program," *American Economic Review* 91, no. 2
     (May 2001): 145–149; Angela L. Duckworth and Martin E.P. Seligman, "Self-
     Discipline Outdoes IQ in Predicting Academic Performance of Adolescents,"
     Psychological Science 16, no. 12 (December 2005): 939–944; Giorgio Brunello
     and Martin Schlotter, *The Effect of Noncognitive Skills and Personality Traits
     on Labour Market Outcomes: Analytical Report for the European Commission
     Prepared by the European Expert Network on Economics of Education
     (EENEE)* (Munich: EENEE, 2010), https://www.researchgate.net/publication
     /45436342_The_Effect_of_Non_Cognitive_Skills_and_Personality_Traits_on_
     Labour_Market_Outcomes.

6   Organisation for Economic Co-operation and Development, *Teachers Matter:
     Attracting, Developing and Retaining Effective Teachers* (Paris: OECD
     Publishing, 2005): 99–100.

7   Maurice J. Elias et al., *Promoting Social and Emotional Learning: Guidelines
     for Educators* (Virginia: Association for Supervision and Curriculum
     Development, 1997).

8   Toronto District School Board, *Children and Youth: Mental Health and
     Well-Being; Strategic Plan—An Overview—Year 2; Years of Action 2013–2017,
     Toronto District School Board* (Toronto: Toronto District School Board, 2014),
     http://www.tdsb.on.ca/Portals/0/Elementary/docs/SupportingYou/
     MentalHealthStrategyOverview.pdf.

9   Daniel Hamlin and Joseph Flessa, "Parental Involvement Initiatives: An
     Analysis," *Educational Policy*, October 19, 2016, https://doi.
     org/10.1177/0895904816673739.

10   John Bridgeland, Mary Bruce and Arya Hariharan, *The Missing Piece: A
     National Teacher Survey on How Social and Emotional Learning Can Empower
     Children and Transform Schools; A Report for CASEL* (Washington, D.C.:
     Civic Enterprises, 2013).

11   Joseph Durlak et al., "The Impact of Enhancing Students' Social and Emotional Learning: A Meta-analysis of School-Based Universal Interventions."

12   Gillian Parekh, *A Case for Inclusive Education* (Toronto: Toronto District School Board, 2013), http://www.autismontario.com/client/aso/ao.nsf/docs/8075 69f8d21a5bca85257c65005e5258/$file/inclusion_1.pdf.

13   Tracy Sherlock, "B.C. School Districts Adopt Unique Strategies to Help Students Stay Alert," *The Vancouver Sun*, September 3, 2013, http://www. vancouversun.com/health/school+districts+adopt+unique+strategies+help+ students+stay+alert/8860653/story.html.

14   Joseph Durlak et al., "The Impact of Enhancing Students' Social and Emotional Learning: A Meta-analysis of School-Based Universal Interventions."

15   Carol S. Dweck, *Mindset: The New Psychology of Success* (New York: Random House, 2006).

16   Jeannie Brooks, *Keeping Track: How Schools Structure Inequality* (New Haven: Yale University Press, 1985); John Hattie, *Visible Learning: A Synthesis of Over 800 Meta-analyses Relating to Achievement* (London: Routledge, 2009); Eric Hanushek and Ludger Woessmann, "Does Educational Tracking Affect Performance and Inequality? Differences-in-Differences Evidence across Countries," *National Bureau of Economic Research*, Working Paper No. 11124 (February 2005): 1–31; For Canadian research, see Bruce Curtis, D.W. Livingstone and Harry Smaller, *Stacking the Deck: The Streaming of Working-Class Kids in Ontario Schools* (Toronto: Our Schools/Our Selves Educational Foundation, 1992); Harvey Krahn and Alison Taylor, "'Streaming' in the 10th Grade in Four Canadian Provinces in 2000," *Education Matters: Insights on Education, Learning and Training in Canada* 4, no. 2, (June 2007): 16–26, Statistics Canada, no. 81-004-XIE.

17   Organisation for Economic Co-operation and Development, *Equity and Quality in Education: Supporting Disadvantaged Students and Schools* (Paris: OECD Publishing, 2012), 56.

18   Cited in Daniel Hamlin and David Cameron, *Applied or Academic: High Impact Decisions for Ontario Students* (Toronto: People for Education, 2015).

19   Marguerite del Giudice, "Grit Trumps Talent and IQ: A Story Every Parent (and Educator) Should Read," *National Geographic*, October 14, 2014, http://news.nationalgeographic.com/news/2014/10/141015-angela-duckworth-success-grit-psychology-self-control-science-nginnovators.

20   Thomas Toch and Susan Headden, "How to Motivate Students to Work Harder," *The Atlantic*, September 3, 2014, http://www.theatlantic.com/ education/archive/2014/09/how-to-get-insecure-students-to-work-harder/379500.

21   David Yaeger, Ken Walton and Carol Dweck. "A Note About Coverage of Mindset Research in the *Atlantic*," *Adolescent Development Research Group*, Department of Psychology, College of Liberal Arts, University of Texas

at Austin, September 18, 2014, http://labs.la.utexas.edu/adrg/2014/09/18/
note-about-coverage-of-mindset-research-in-the-atlantic.

22   Jeffrey D. Burke and Rolf Loeber, "The Effectiveness of the Stop Now and Plan
      (SNAP) Program for Boys at Risk for Violence and Delinquency," *Prevention
      Science* 16, no. 2 (February 2015): 242–253.

23   Marc D. Lewis et al., "Changes in the Neural Bases of Emotion Regulation
      Associated with Clinical Improvement in Children with Behavior Problems,"
      Development and Psychopathology 20, no. 3 (July 2008): 913–939; Steven
      Woltering et al., "Neural Changes Associated with Treatment Outcome in
      Children with Externalizing Problems," *Biological Psychiatry* 70, no. 9
      (November 2011): 873–879.

24   Rebecca Godfrey, *Under the Bridge: The True Story of the Murder of Reena
      Virk* (Toronto: HarperCollins, 2005); David Cullen, *Columbine* (New York:
      Twelve, 2009).

25   British Columbia Performance Standards for Social Responsibility, *Social
      Responsibility: October 2001; A Framework* (British Columbia: British Columbia
      Ministry of Education, 2001), https://www.bced.gov.bc.ca/perf_stands/sintro.pdf.

CHAPTER FOUR: TECHNOLOGY: VOICE, INFLUENCE AND
DIGITAL CITIZENSHIP

1   Andreas Schleicher, "GEIS 2016—Dinner remarks," speech, Global Education
      Industry Summit, 2016, www.oecd.org/edu/ceri/GEIS2016-Dinner-speech.pdf.

2   Mark Koba, "Education Tech Funding Soars—But Is It Working in the
      Classroom?," *Fortune*, April 28, 2015, http://fortune.com/2015/04/28/education-
      tech-funding-soars-but-is-it-working-in-the-classroom.

3   Futuresource Consulting Ltd., *Technology in Education: Global Trends,
      Universal Spend and Market Outlook* (Hertfordshire, U.K.: Futuresource
      Consulting Ltd., 2014).

4   Partnership for 21st Century Skills, *P21 Framework Definitions* (Washington,
      D.C.: Partnership for 21st Century Skills, 2009), http://www.p21.org/storage/
      documents/P21_Framework_Definitions.pdf.

5   Nick Rockel, "Tom Chau Is Giving Disabled Children the Tools to Speak
      Out," *The Globe and Mail*, November 2, 2010.

6   "Learning Unleashed: Where Governments Are Failing to Provide Youngsters
      with a Decent Education, the Private Sector is Stepping In," *The Economist*,
      August 1, 2015, 19–22.

7   Nicholas Negroponte, "What Technology Wants Vs. What People Want,"
      (Speech, Techonomy Conference, Lake Tahoe, CA, August 6, 2010),
      https://www.youtube.com/watch?v=2rz2yhkahMo&nohtml5=False.

8   Mark Warschauer and Morgan Ames, "Can One Laptop Per Child Save
      the World's Poor?," *Journal of International Affairs* 64, no. 1 (Fall/Winter
      2010): 37.

9   Ontario Ministry of Education, *Me Read? No Way! A Practical Guide to Improving Boys' Literacy Skills* (Queen's Printer for Ontario, 2004), http://edu.gov.on.ca/eng/document/brochure/meread/meread.pdf.

10 New Media Horizons and Consortium on School Networking. *The NMC/CoSN Horizon Report: 2016 K–12 Edition* (Austin, T.X.: The New Media Consortium, 2016).

11 Lucinda Gray, Nina Thomas and Laurie Lewis, *Teachers' Use of Educational Technology in U.S. Public Schools: 2009* (Washington, D.C.: National Center for Education Statistics, 2010).

12 Organisation for Economic Co-operation and Development, *Students, Computers and Learning: Making the Connection* (Paris: OECD Publishing, 2015), http://www.keepeek.com/Digital-Asset-Management/oecd/education/students-computers-and-learning_9789264239555-en#.WPgs6f21u8U.

13 The Ontario Library Association, Queen's University and People for Education, *School Libraries and Student Achievement in Ontario* (Toronto: Ontario Library Association, 2006).

14 Kelly Gallagher-Mackay and People for Education, *Broader Measures of Success: Measuring What Matters in Education* (Toronto: People for Education, 2013), 12, http://peopleforeducation.ca/measuring-what-matters/wp-content/uploads/2013/10/P4E-MWM-full-report-2013.pdf.

15 Literacy and Numeracy Secretariat, *Learning Blocks for Literacy and Numeracy* (Toronto: Literacy and Numeracy Secretariat, 2007), www.curriculum.org/secretariat/files/May30LearningBlocks.pdf.

16 Ontario Ministry of Education, *Achieving Excellence: A Renewed Vision for Education in Ontario* (Queen's Printer for Ontario, 2014).

17 Michael Fullan, *Great to Excellent: Launching the Next Stage of Ontario's Education Agenda* (Toronto: Government of Ontario, 2013), http://www.michaelfullan.ca/wp-content/uploads/2013/09/13_Fullan_Great-to-Excellent.pdf.

18 Richard Rotherstein, Rebecca Jacobsen and Tamara Wilder, *Grading Education: Getting Accountability Right* (Washington, D.C./New York: Economic Policy Institute/Teachers College Press, 2008); William A. Firestone and David Mayrowetz, "Rethinking 'High Stakes': Lessons from the United States and England and Wales," *Teachers College Record* 102, no. 4 (2000): 724–749; Carol A. Barnes, *Standards Reform in High-Poverty Schools: Managing Conflict and Building Capacity* (New York: Teachers College Press, 2002); Gail Sunderman, James Kim and Gary Orfield, *NCLB Meets School Realities: Lessons from the Field* (Thousand Oaks, CA: Corwin Press, 2005); Sharon L. Nichols and David C. Berliner, *Collateral Damage: How High-Stakes Testing Corrupts America's Schools* (Cambridge, MA: Harvard Education Press, 2007); Laura S. Hamilton, Brian M. Stetcher and Kun Yuan, *Standards-Based Reform in the United States: History, Research and Future Directions* (Santa Monica, CA: RAND Corporation, 2008), www.rand.org/content/dam/rand/pubs/reprints/2009/RAND_RP1384.pdf.

19   Helen Raptis, "Ending the Reign of the Fraser Institute's School Rankings," *Canadian Journal of Education* 35, no. 1 (2012): 187–201.

20   Ontario Teachers' Federation et al., *A New Vision for Large-Scale Testing in Ontario* (Toronto: Ontario Teachers' Federation, 2011), www.otffeo.on.ca/wp-content/uploads/sites/2/2013/09/new_vision.pdf; Elementary Teachers' Federation of Ontario, *Adjusting the Optics: Assessment, Evaluation and Reporting; A Response from the Elementary Teachers' Federation of Ontario* (Toronto: Elementary Teachers' Federation of Ontario, 2001), http://www.etfo.ca/Publications/PositionPapers/Documents/Adjusting%20the%20Optics%20-%20Assessment,%20Evaluation%20and%20Reporting.pdf; "Issues Related to Provincial Achievement Tests: What Parents Need to Know," Alberta Teachers' Association, accessed March 20, 2017, https://www.teachers.ab.ca/Publications/The%20Learning%20Team/Volume%2012/Number4/Pages/IssuesrelatedtoProvincialAchievementTests.aspx; "Foundation Skills Assessment," British Columbia Teachers' Federation, accessed March 20, 2017, https://bctf.ca/fsa.aspx.

21   Diane Ravitch, *The Death and Life of the Great American School System: How Testing and Choice Are Undermining Education* (New York: Basic Books, 2010); For Canadian research, see Louis Volante, "Educational Quality and Accountability in Ontario: Past, Present and Future," *Canadian Journal of Educational Administration and Policy* 58 (January 2007), https://eric.ed.gov/?id=EJ806973.

22   Andreas Schleicher, "Can Competencies Assessed by PISA Be Considered the Fundamental School Knowledge 15-Year-Olds Should Possess?," *Journal of Educational Change* 8, no. 4 (July 2007): 350; For Canadian perspectives, see Kadriye Ercikan, Maria Elena Oliveri and Debra Sandilands, "Large-Scale Assessments of Achievement in Canada," in *International Guide to Student Achievement*, ed. John Mattie and Eric M. Anderson (New York, Routledge, 2012), 456–459; Don A. Klinger, Christopher DeLuca and Tess Miller, "The Evolving Culture of Large-Scale Assessments in Canadian Education," *Canadian Journal of Educational Administration and Policy* 76 (July 2008).

23   "About the Project," People for Education, accessed March 6, 2017, http://peopleforeducation.ca/measuring-what-matters/about-the-project.

24   People for Education, *Measuring What Matters: Progress Report; Phase 3: 2015–2016* (Toronto: People for Education, 2016), 14, http://peopleforeducation.ca/measuring-what-matters/wp-content/uploads/2016/11/P4E-MWM-Phase-3-report-2016.pdf

CHAPTER FIVE: SCHOOLS OF CHOICE

1   J. Douglas Willms, *The Case for Universal French Instruction* (Fredericton, N.B.: Canadian Research Institute for Social Policy), 2008.

2   Rob Brown and Gillian Parekh, *Programs in the TDSB: An Overview 2011–2013* (Toronto: Toronto District School Board, n.d.).

3   Justine S. Hastings, Christopher A. Neilson and Seth D. Zimmerman, "The Effect of School Choice on Intrinsic Motivation and Academic Outcomes," *NBER Working Paper Series* 18324 (2012): 36; Caroline M. Hoxby, "Does Competition among Public Schools Benefit Students and Taxpayers?", *American Economic Review* 90 (2000): 1209–38; Jack Buckley and Mark Schneider, *Charter Schools: Hype or Hope?* (Princeton, N.J.: Princeton University Press, 2009).

4   Erhan Sinay, *Programs of Choice in the TDSB: Characteristics of Students in French Immersion, Alternative Schools and Other Specialized Schools and Programs* (Toronto: Toronto District School Board, 2010), http://www.tdsb. on.ca/Portals/0/community/community%20advisory%20committees/fslac/support%20staff/programsofchoicestudentcharacteristics.pdf.

5   Xiao Pang, Michael Kozlow and W. Todd Rogers. "An Analysis of Questionnaire and Contextual Data for Grade 9 Students in Academic and Applied Mathematics Courses" (Toronto, O.N.: EQAO Research, 2012).

6   James Croll and Patricia Lee, *Report of the French Second Language Commission: A Comprehensive Review of French Second Language Programs and Services Within the Anglophone Sector of the New Brunswick Department of Education* (Fredericton: Government of New Brunswick, 2008), http://www.unb.ca/fredericton/second-language/_resources/pdf/fsleview/fslreporteng.pdf.

7   J. Douglas Willms, *The Case for Universal French Instruction*.

8   Max Cooke, "A Collision of Culture, Values and Education Policy: Scrapping Early French Immersion in New Brunswick," *Education Canada* 49, no. 2 (Spring 2009): 46–50, http://www.cea-ace.ca/sites/cea-ace.ca/files/EdCan-2009-v49-n2-Cooke.pdf.

9   *Small & Ryan v. New Brunswick (Minister of Education)*, S/M/32/08, 2008 NBQB 201, CanLII, http://canlii.ca/t/1x6r8.

10 Andrew Cromwell, "Early French Immersion Changes Continue to Spark Opposition in NB," *Global News,* November 16, 2016, http://globalnews.ca/news/3071213/early-french-immersion-changes-continue-to-spark-opposition-in-nb.

CHAPTER SIX: SCHOOLS CAN'T DO IT ALONE

1   Richard Rothstein, "Whose Problem Is Poverty?," *Educational Leadership* 65, no. 7 (April 2008): 8–13, http://www.ascd.org/publications/educational-leadership/apr08/vol65/num07/Whose-Problem-Is-Poverty%C2%A2.aspx.

2   Toronto Community Health Profiles Partnership, *Toronto Health Profiles: CPA 851* (2001–2016), based on the 2006 census.

3 People for Education, *Making Connections Beyond School Walls: People for Education Annual Report on Ontario's Publicly Funded Schools 2012* (Toronto: People for Education, 2012), http://www.peopleforeducation.ca/wp-content/uploads/2012/05/Annual-Report-2012-web.pdf.

4 John Carlisle, *Coroner's Inquest Touching the Death of Ashley Smith* (Toronto, O.N.: Correctional Service Canada, 2013), www.csc-scc.gc.ca/publications/005007-9009-eng.shtml; Josh Wingrove, "Official response to Ashley Smith case sidesteps most prison proposals," *The Globe and Mail*, December 12, 2014, http://www.theglobeandmail.com/news/politics/official-response-to-ashley-smith-case-sidesteps-most-prison-proposals/article22074448.

5 *Reducing the risk, addressing the need* (Fredericton, N.B.: Government of New Brunswick), retrieved April 10, 2017, http://www2.gnb.ca/content/dam/gnb/Departments/jus/PDF/publications/ReducingRisk.pdf; Ombudsman and Child and Youth Advocate, *The Ashley Smith Report* (Fredericton, N.B.: Government of New Brunswick, 2008), www.cyanb.ca/images/AshleySmith-e.pdf; Ombudsman and Child and Youth Advocate, *Connecting the Dots: A report on the condition of youth-at-risk and youth with very complex needs in New Brunswick* (Fredericton, N.B.: Government of New Brunswick, 2008), https://www.ombudnb.ca/site/images/PDFs/ConnectingtheDots-e.pdf.

6 Paule Langevin and Patricia Lamarre, "Community Learning Centers in Quebec: Changing Lives, Changing Communities," in *Developing Community Schools, Community Learning Centers, Extended-service Schools and Multi-service Schools: International Exemplars for Practice, Policy and Research*, ed. Hal Lawson and Dolf van Veen (Dordrecht: Springer, 2016).

CHAPTER SEVEN: THE CHILDREN WE SHARE

1 Joyce L. Epstein, "School/Family/Community Partnerships: Caring for the Children We Share," *Phi Delta Kappan* 76, no. 9 (May 1995): 701.

2 Ontario Physical Health and Education Association, *Our Kids Are on Fast Forward: Why Is Our Health and Physical Education Curriculum Stuck on Pause?* (Toronto: Ontario Physical Health and Education Association, 2013), 4.

3 Louise Brown, "Educators Battle False Information as Sex-Ed Opposition Grows," *Toronto Star*, April 26, 2015.

4 Thorncliffe Parents Association's Facebook page, accessed September 15, 2015, https://www.facebook.com/thorncliffeparents.

5 Anthony Bryk and Barbara Schneider, *Trust in Schools: A Core Resource for Improvement* (New York: Russell Sage Foundation, 2002).

6 Marcus Gee, "Solving the refugee crisis is pretty simple for these kids," *The Globe and Mail*, September 25, 2015, http://www.theglobeandmail.com/news/national/solving-the-refugee-crisis-is-pretty-simple-for-these-kids/article26551810.

CHAPTER EIGHT: IT'S ALL ABOUT THE TEACHER

1   Pasi Sahlberg, "Myth: You Can Do More with Less," *Alberta Teachers' Association Magazine,* June 1, 2015, https://www.teachers.ab.ca/Publications/ATA%20Magazine/Volume%2095%202014-15/Number-4/Pages/Myth-Pasi-Sahlberg.aspx.

2   Ronald F. Ferguson, "Paying for Public Education: New Evidence on How and Why Money Matters," *Harvard Journal on Legislation* 28, no. 2 (1991): 465–498; Steven G. Rivkin, Eric A. Hanushek and John F. Kain, "Teachers, Schools and Academic Achievement," *Econometrica* 73, no. 2 (March 2005): 417–458; Paul S. Wright, Sandra P. Horn and William L. Sanders, "Teacher and Classroom Context Effects on Student Achievement: Implications for Teacher Evaluation," *Journal of Personnel Evaluation in Education* 11, no. 1 (April 1997): 57–67.

3   Thomas J. Kane, Kerri A. Kerr and Robert C. Pianta, eds., *Designing Teacher Evaluation Systems: New Guidance from the Measures of Effective Teaching Project* (San Francisco: Jossey-Bass, 2014), http://k12education.gates foundation.org/wp-content/uploads/2015/11/Designing-Teacher-Evaluation-Systems_freePDF.pdf.

4   Organisation for Economic Co-operation and Development, *Teachers Matter: Attracting, Developing and Retaining Effective Teachers.*

5   Rachel Mendleson, "Why It's So Hard to Fire Bad Teachers," *Maclean's,* July 8, 2009, http://www.macleans.ca/news/canada/why-its-so-hard-to-fire-bad-teachers.

6   Doug Hart and Arlo Kempf, *Public Attitudes toward Education in Ontario 2015: The 19th OISE Survey of Educational Issues* (Toronto: Ontario Institute for Studies in Education of the University of Toronto, 2015), http://www.oise.utoronto.ca/oise/UserFiles/Media/Media_Relations/Final_Report_-_19th_OISE_Survey_on_Educational_Issues_2015.pdf.

7   Robert Benzie, "Ontario Teachers' Labour Dispute: Poll Suggests Nearly 50 Percent of Ontarians Believe Unions' Tactics Ineffective," *Toronto Star,* November 30, 2012.

8   "Neither Side is Winning the Battle for Public Opinion in BC Teachers' Dispute," *Ipsos,* September 10, 2014, http://www.ipsos-na.com/news-polls/pressrelease.aspx?id=6595.

9   Janet French, "Alberta Teacher Admits Humiliating Red Deer Students, Writing on Their Faces," *Edmonton Journal,* April 12, 2016, http://edmontonjournal.com/news/local-news/alberta-teacher-admits-humiliating-red-deer-students; "Red Deer Teacher Who Humiliated Students Can't Teach for 6 Months," *Canadian Press,* April 15, 2016, http://www.edmontonsun.com/2016/04/15/red-deer-teacher-who-humiliated-students-cant-teach-for-6-months; Janet French, "'He Treated You like . . . an Idiot': Alberta Teacher Humiliated Students by Writing Reminders on Their Foreheads," *National*

Post, April 12, 2016, http://news.nationalpost.com/news/canada/he-treated-you-like-an-idiot-alberta-teacher-humiliated-students-by-writing-reminders-on-their-foreheads; Janice Johnston, "Red Deer Teacher Who Humiliated Students Found Guilty of Misconduct," *CBC News*, April 12, 2016, http://www.cbc.ca/news/canada/edmonton/red-deer-teacher-who-humiliated-students-found-guilty-of-misconduct-1.3532765; Troy Gillard, "ATA Disciplines Red Deer Teacher Who Bullied Students," April 13, 2016, http://rdnewsnow.com/article/499284/ata-disciplines-red-deer-teacher-who-bullied-students.

10   "Red Deer Teacher Who Humiliated Students Can't Teach for 6 Months," *Canadian Press*.

11   "Teacher Resigns for Humiliating Students," *Red Deer Advocate*, April 13, 2016, http://www.reddeeradvocate.com/news/Teacher_resigns_for_humiliating_students_375498571.html.

12   Statistics Canada; Council of Ministers of Education, Canada; and Tourism and the Centre for Education Statistics, *Education Indicators in Canada: An International Perspective 2014* (Canadian Education Statistics Council, 2015), http://www.cmec.ca/Publications/Lists/Publications/Attachments/342/PCEIP-International-Report-2014-EN.pdf.

13   Organisation for Economic Co-operation and Development, *Pisa 2015: Results in Focus*.

14   Statistics Canada; Council of Ministers of Education, Canada; and Tourism and the Centre for Education Statistics, *Education Indicators in Canada: An International Perspective 2014*.

15   Government of Singapore, *Analysis of Revenue and Expenditure: Financial Year 2015* (Singapore: Government of Singapore, 2015), http://www.singaporebudget.gov.sg/data/budget_2015/download/FY2015_Analysis_of_Revenue_and_Expenditure.pdf.

16   "General Government Expenditure by Function: The Share of Social Protection in General Government Expenditure Grew in 2013," Statistics Finland, published January 30, 2015, http://www.stat.fi/til/jmete/2013/jmete_2013_2015-01-30_tie_001_en.html.

17   "Government Expenditure on Education, Total (% of GDP)," United Nations Educational, Scientific and Cultural Organisation (UNESCO) Institute for Statistics, The World Bank Group, accessed March 10, 2017, http://data.worldbank.org/indicator/SE.XPD.TOTL.GD.ZS; Canadian Institute for Health Information, *National Health Expenditure Trends, 1975 to 2016* (Ottawa, Canadian Institute for Health Information, 2016), https://www.cihi.ca/sites/default/files/document/nhex-trends-narrative-report_2016_en.pdf; Canadian Institute for Health Information, *National Heath Expenditure Trends, 1975-2015: Chartbook* (Ottawa: Canadian Institute for Health Information, 2015), https://www.cihi.ca/sites/default/files/document/2015-nhex_chartbook_en.pdf.

18   Pasi Sahlberg, *Finnish Lessons 2.0: What Can the World Learn from Education Change in Finland?*, 2nd ed. (New York: Teachers College Press, 2015).

19   "Pupil-Teacher Ratio in Primary Education (Headcount Basis)," United Nations Educational, Scientific and Cultural Organisation (UNESCO) Institute for Statistics, The World Bank Group, accessed March 10, 2017, http://data.worldbank.org/indicator/SE.PRM.ENRL.TC.ZS; "Pupil-Teacher Ratio— Primary in Singapore," *Trading Economics*, accessed March 10, 2017, http://www.tradingeconomics.com/singapore/pupil-teacher-ratio-primary-wb-data.html.

20   Organisation for Economic Co-operation and Development, *Finland: Key Findings from the Teaching and Learning International Survey (TALIS)* (Paris, OECD Publishing, n.d.), https://www.oecd.org/finland/TALIS-2013-country-note-Finland.pdf; Organisation for Economic Co-operation and Development, *Singapore: Key Findings from the Teaching and Learning International Survey (TALIS)* (Paris, OECD Publishing, n.d.), https://www.oecd.org/edu/school/TALIS-2013-country-note-Singapore.pdf; Organisation for Economic Co-operation and Development, *Alberta (Canada): Key Findings from the Teaching and Learning International Survey (TALIS)* (Paris, OECD Publishing, n.d.), https://www.oecd.org/canada/TALIS-2013-country-note-Alberta-Canada.pdf.

INDEX

Abby (Regina student), 49
academic curriculum, 88
Alberta
  collective agreements in, 217
  curriculum changes in, 31
  strikes by teachers in, 218
  teachers' union in, 215–22
Alberta Initiative for School
  Improvement (AISI), 222
Alberta Teachers' Association (ATA),
  215–22
All Our Futures (Robinson et al.),
  50–51
alternative schools and programs,
  129–32, 144, 146, 151, 157
Ames, Martin, 115–16
Amini, Mahta, 203–4
anglophone schools, 180–82
Anwar (George Webster student),
  28–29
anxiety
  coping strategies, 86
  experienced by Naaz, 85–86

experienced by Sam, 179
  in students, 74, 99
applied curriculum, 88
  for First Nations, 146–47
arts
  and creativity, 65
  importance of, 65
  student involvement in, 66–67
  support for, 66–67
Au, John, 151, 152
Augimeri, Dr. Leena, 93
autism, 167–68, 169
  Mohammed's story, 76–80
AvRuskin, Hayley, 113–14
Ayube, Rehanna, 23, 27

Beghetto, Ronald, 51
Booi, Larry, 221
Bowles, Samuel, 72–73
British Columbia
  MindUP, 98–99
  Second Step, 99–100
  SEL-BC, 100–101

social-emotional skills and
learning, 95–96, 100–103
social responsibility performance
standards, 96–100
teacher education in social-
emotional skills, 100
Brodie, Jennifer, 203
Brookings Institute, 139
bullying, 96

Cajete, Dr. Gregory, 184
Calm, Alert, and Learning (Shanker),
81
Cambridge Education, 212
Cameron, David, 139
Campaign Life Coalition, 195, 200
Camp Oochigeas, 66
Canadian Achievement Test
and Radical Math program, 31
Canadian Council of Chief
Executives, 14, 17
Canadian Families Alliance, 195
Canadian Parents for French, 155
Cape Breton University, 6, 184
Carrillo, Rolando, 94–95
Cary-Meagher, Sheila, 21
C.D. Howe Institute, 15
Centre for Real-World Learning,
52–53, 55
Centre for Urban Schooling, 23
Charland, Nathalie, 119–20, 121
charter schools, 144
Chau, Tom, 109–11, 112
Chechile, Michael, 117, 118–19, 122
Child Development Institute (CDI),
93, 94, 175
child poverty

in Toronto District School Board,
20
Chloe (Regina student), 45
Christina (George Webster student),
164–66, 171
Cindrich School, 80–87, 95
Cioata, Corvin, 108–9, 110, 111–12,
113, 114, 116, 133
Citizens for Educational Choice, 155
City View Alternative School, 129
collaboration
teaching of/importance of, 16–17
communication skills
teaching of, 16–17
communication techniques
for students with disabilities,
109–12
community and school relationship,
173–85
Community Learning Centres
(CLCs), 180–82
Conference Board of Canada, 17
Connery, Susan, 119, 120–21, 122, 126
Connie (Granite Ridge student),
89, 90
Corke, Steve, 23, 26–27, 34
Coyle, Robyn, 23, 34
Crane, Jeff, 194–95, 196, 197–98, 199,
200, 201
creativity
and the arts, 65
assessing/measuring, 51, 52–55
challenges in fostering, 47–48
definition, 50
and extracurricular activities,
65
habits or traits of, 53, 55

importance of, 49–51, 68
methods for supporting, 46,
47–49
nurturing, 58–62
questions about, 51
results of encouraging, 64
teaching of, 16–17
critical thinking skills
fostering, 4–5, 133, 157
in IB program, 151, 152, 157
importance of, 68
negative aspect to, 73
taxonomy of, 22
teaching of, 16–17
Croll, Jim, 153, 154
Cross Country Checkup, 14

Dalhousie University, 6
Daman (Cindrich School student),
83, 84–85, 103
Dewey, Ken, 95
Dewson Street Public School
diversity of neighbourhood,
189–90
and refugee sponsorship, 202–6
Dianne (Mi'kmaw elder), 38–39
disabilities, students with
communication techniques,
109–12
mobility of, 113
discipline: during recess and lunch, 24
diversity
in Dewson Street, 189–90
in George Webster, 170
in Monarch Park, 150
and schools of choice, 146–47
in St. Stephen, 177

in textbooks, 125–26
in Thorncliffe Park, 192–93
"Do Schools Kill Creativity?"
(Robinson TED talk), 49
Douglas Park Elementary School, 45
dropouts, preventing, 5
Dr. Paul Steinhauer Pediatric Clinic,
176
Dunfield, Alan, 177
Dweck, Carol, 87, 89, 92
dyslexia: Connie's story, 89–90

Eckstein, Bob, 177–78, 180
Education for Democracy in a
Digital Age (EDDA), 128
Education Quality and
Accountability Office (EQAO),
134, 135
Elias, Maurice J., 74
Enhanced Learning Program, 143–44
enrichment programs: Yasotharan
in, 3–4
Esmonde, Indigo, 23
Essabhai, Rahim, 59, 210
Evergreen Elementary School, 119–20,
126
expectations, effect of low on students,
34–35
extracurricular activities, 58, 65

family. *See also* parents
role in teaching social-emotional
skills, 73–74
Ferguson, Dr. Ronald, 212, 213
Finland, 223, 224, 225–26, 227
First Nations. *See also* Mi'kmaw
Kina'matnewey (MK)

graduation rates, 5
math teaching for Mi'kmaw
   students, 38–40
Mi'kmaw education system, 6–7
and Nova Scotia education
   system, 36–40
post-secondary education of,
   6–7
prejudices against, 5
programs available to, 146, 147
and residential schools, 36
school and community relationship in, 183–84
Flahat, Aiman, 55–56, 57, 59, 60,
   63, 64
4Cs, 16–17
Fraser Institute, 150
Fraser Mustard Early Learning
   Academy, 193
Free the Children, 150
French Immersion, 145, 146, 147–48,
   153–56
Fullan, Michael, 135

The Gates Foundation, 211
Genius Hour, 46, 47–49, 48, 210, 211
George Webster Elementary School,
   13
and community, 164
description of, 17–18
diversity at, 170
impressive nature of, 136
math teaching at, 22–24
medical services at, 175–76
and Model Schools initiative, 19–20
multicultural nature of, 18, 23
parent involvement at, 169–72

Radical Math group and program,
   22–31
recess and lunch problems, 24
relationship with community,
   173–76
reputation of, 167
SNAP program at, 92–95
socio-economic status, 18–19
and teacher expectations, 35
teaching methods at, 33
gifted programs, 144, 149, 157
Gintis, Herbert, 72–73
Google, 46
Google Apps for Education (GAFE), 124
graduation rates, of First Nations
   students, 5, 40
Graham, Brittany, 145, 146, 147
Granite Ridge Education Centre
   (GREC), 87–91, 95
Grant, Devin, 66–67
Grounds, Debbie, 77, 78–79
growth mindset, 87–92

Harris, Mike, 216
health concerns, 174–76
Heckman, James, 73
Heritage Canada, 180
Hewko, Hannah, 204
Highet, Heather, 88, 89, 90, 91
Hill, Tessa, 129–30, 131–32, 133
Holland Bloorview Kids
   Rehabilitation Hospital,
   109–10, 114
home life, effects on students, 85–86
The Hospital for Sick Children, 63,
   93, 161
Hymel, Shelley, 96, 100

Infinity Lab, 109, 111, 112, 113, 114

innovation, importance of, 68

Innovation and Inquiry in the
   Classroom (Juliani), 46

integrative thinking, 57, 58, 60, 68.
   See also I-Think

International Baccalaureate (IB),
   144, 145, 150–51, 157

Internet safety, 116–17, 118–19

Isaac (Regina student), 45, 48–49

Ismaili, Eid, 193–94, 196, 197, 198–99,
   200, 201

I-Think, 58–64, 68, 210

James, Jason, 77, 78–79

Jarrett (Owen Sound student), 146,
   147

Jarvis Collegiate, 60

Jenkins, Anne, 119, 120, 121

John Polanyi Collegiate Institute,
   3–4
   creativity success at, 64
   crime in neighbourhood, 57
   demographics of, 56–57
   I-Think program at, 59–64
   mission of, 57, 61
   project to increase enrolment,
      60–63
   socio-economic makeup of
      community, 56–57

Juliani, A.J., 46

Kahne, Joseph, 127

Kaufman, James, 51

Kidder, Annie, 136, 139, 140

Kisko, Carla, 205

Knezevic, Bogdan, 143–44, 145

Kornberg, Nogah, 59, 61

Kurdi, Alan, 201

Lafley, Alan, 58

Langevin, Paule, 180, 181

Learning Metrics Task Force, 139

Learning: The Treasure Within
   (UNESCO report), 16

Lee, Patricia, 153, 154

Lee-Chin, Michael, 58

Leps, Caroline, 66

Lester B. Pearson School Board,
   116–17, 122–23, 124–25, 126

literacy
   and computer use, 121
   teaching methods, 33–34

lunch, problems during, 24

Lunney Borden, Lisa, 36–38, 40, 210

MacArthur Foundation, 127

MacKinnon, Rob, 150, 151, 152

Madeira, Jimmy, 93

Manley, John, 14

Manning, Bev, 220

Mappin-Kasirer, Benjamin, 71–72

Marshall, Donald Jr., 36

Martin, Roger, 57–58, 62–63, 67–68

mathematics
   Canadian test scores in, 14
   core skills/rote learning *vs.*
      concepts/discovery debate,
      13, 14–15, 31–34
   criticism of teaching methods,
      14–15
   destreaming, 89–91
   and growth mindset, 88–91
   improvement in test scores, 31

and Mi'kmaw language, 37
Radical Math program, 22–31
"Show Me Your Math" program,
    38–40
standards in Ontario, 15–16
teaching changes at George
    Webster, 22–24
McBride, Lianne, 80–87, 101, 210, 211
McGuinty, Dalton, 135
McIntyre, Ray, 23
McLellan, Justice Hugh, 155
McVety, Charles, 192
Measuring Effective Teaching (MET)
    project, 211–12
"Measuring What Matters," 138–40
Meldrum, Kim, 119, 122
mental health, 175. See also social-
    emotional skills
    parents' desire to support, 74–75
    role of schools in aiding, 75
    services in New Brunswick,
        177–78
Mental Health Commission of
    Canada, 103
mentoring: Yasotharan and, 4
Mi'kmaw communities, 183–84
    education in Nova Scotia, 36–40
Mi'kmaw Kina'matnewey (MK), 6–7,
    13, 36–41, 183, 210
Mindset Works (website), 89
MindUP, 98–99
Mitra, Sugata, 114–15
Model School for Inner Cities
    initiative
    funding for, 20–21
    at George Webster, 19, 20, 22–23,
        172–76, 210

and Parent Academy program, 167
vision and methods, 20
Mohammed (George Webster stu-
    dent), 76–80
Monarch Park Collegiate, 150–53, 157
Morris, Dale, 23
multiculturalism. See also diversity
    at George Webster, 18, 23

Naaz (Cindrich School student),
    85–86
Nastoh, Hamed, 96
National Center for Education
    Statistics (NCES), 122
Negroponte, John, 115
New Brunswick
    French Immersion in, 153–56
    and mental health services,
        177–78
    and schools of choice challenges,
        153–56
Nichols, Jon, 52
"non-cognitive" skills, 72. See also
    social-emotional skills
Nova Scotia. See also Mi'kmaw
    Kina'matnewey (MK)
    First Nations education in, 36–40
    graduation rates, 40
Nurturing Creativity in the Classroom
    (Kaufman and Beghetto), 51

Oakland Unified School District,
    128
1000 School Challenge, 203, 205
Ontario
    focus on test scores, 134–35
    math standards in, 15–16

parental involvement in schools,
189–206
sex education controversy, 192–201
teachers' unions in, 216
work to rule tactic, 218
Ontario College of Teachers, 216
Ontario Institute for Studies in
Education (oise), 23
Organisation of Economic
Co-operation and Development
(OECD), 14, 50, 73, 123
Oxford University. See University of
Oxford

Palmer, Ingrid, 167–72
Parent Academy program, 167, 171
parents
attitudes to schooling, 162
behaviour of, 24–25
concern about sex education
curriculum, 195–201
desire for mental health support,
74–75
and Internet safety, 118–19
involvement of, 24–25, 30, 162–64,
169–72, 189–206
program for, 167
and refugee sponsorship, 202–6
and students' computer skills,
117–18
Partnership for 21st Century Skills,
16–17
Paul, John Jerome, 36, 38, 40,
183–84
Paul, Tiannie, 6–7, 39–40
Pedrini, Lisa, 97–98, 99
Peel District School Board, 143–44

Pelletier, Louis-Georges, 219–20
People for Education, 125, 136,
137–40, 173
playground, and Radical Math
research, 25–31
Polanyi, John, 57
political involvement, by students,
126–29
prejudices, overcoming, 5
Programme for International Student
Assessment (pisa), 15, 135, 223
Promoting Social and Emotional
Learning: Guidelines for
Educators (Elias), 73–74
Prosper, Aaron, 6–7, 39
Prosperity Institute, 67

Quebec
commitment to technology use,
116–17
school and community relationship in, 180–82
Queer Straight Alliance, 130

racism, against Mi'kmaq, 36
recess
problems during, 24
and Radical Math project, 25–31
refugee sponsorship, 201–6
Regent Park, 60
religion: prejudice against Mormons, 5
Rescue Angels Society, 59–60
Rhodes Scholarships, 4, 65–67, 71,
144–45
Right to Play, 30
Robinson, Janice, 202, 204, 206
Robinson, Sir Ken, 49–50, 67

Rosalie (George Webster parenting
worker), 170
Rotman School of Management, 57,
58–59
Rouge National Urban Park, 59

Sam (St. Stephen's student), 178–80
Schleicher, Andreas, 135
school and community relationship
in Eskasoni, 183–84
at George Webster, 173–76
in Quebec, 180–82
at St. Stephen, 176–80
school councils, 190–92
"school in the cloud," 114–16
school ranking/measuring successes,
137–40
schools of choice
appeal to parents, 144–45
and diversity, 146–47
French Immersion, 153–56
negative aspects of, 145–46
New Brunswick experience,
153–56
socio-economic makeup of
students, 145–46
and special needs students, 147
student success in, 145
Schools Welcome Refugees, 203,
205, 206
Scott Mission, 63
Second Step, 99–100
Seerah Mission School, 197, 198
SEL-BC, 100–101
self-regulation
and brain system, 93
Daman's story, 83, 84–85

engine metaphor, 82–83
importance of, 81
Naaz's story, 85–86
and stress, 83–84
sex education, 129–32, 192–201
Shanker, Dr. Stuart, 81, 83
Shaw, Taunya, 82–83
Show Me Your Math program, 38–40
Shubenacadie Indian Residential
School, 36
Singapore, 223, 224, 225, 226–27
Sir William Osler High School, 113
Smith, Ashley, 177
Smith, Mike, 89–90, 91
social-emotional skills. See also
mental health
anxiety in students, 74, 85–86, 99
British Columbia as educational
leader, 100–103
family role in teaching, 73–74
growth mindset, 87–92
importance of, 72–73
and improved learning, 75–76
learned at school, 71–72
MindUP, 98–99
Second Step, 99–100
self-regulation, 80–87
SNAP program, 92–95
social responsibility performance
standards, 96–100
"soft" skills, importance of, 17
Soubry, Bernard, 65–66, 68
Soulé, Helen, 17
specialized programs, 144
special needs students
access improvement for, 156
challenges of, 168

and French Immersion, 147
at George Webster, 76–80, 167, 169
inclusion of, 152
and Infinity Lab, 112–14
in International Baccalaureate
    program, 151
Steinhauer, Dr. Paul, 161–62
St. Francis Xavier University, 37,
    40, 184
Stocker, David, 129, 130, 131, 132, 133
Stokke, Anna, 15, 31–32
Stop Now and Plan (SNAP), 92–95
Strachan, Jacqui, 152
streaming, 35, 56, 62, 88–89, 153
St. Stephen Middle School, 176–77
Students, Computeres and Learning
    (OECD), 123
suicide, 96
Sunny View School, 109, 110, 112,
    113, 114, 133

Taxonomy of the Cognitive Domain
    (Bloom et al.), 22
teachers
    assessment system for, 212–13
    collective agreements in Alberta, 217
    defining high quality, 211–13
    disciplinary hearings, 219–20
    dismissal process, 214–15
    education of, 224
    evaluation of, 226
    and merit pay, 222, 226
    qualities of good, 210
    salaries, 222
    and social-emotional skills, 100
    unions, 213–22
    work to rule, 217–18

technology
    and achievement, 123
    commitment to use in Quebec,
        116–17
    cost of supplying, 115, 124–25, 133
    digital citizenship, 117–18, 126–29
    and Internet safety, 116–17, 118–19
    and learning, 122–23
    and literacy, 121
    one-laptop-per-child projects,
        115–16
    "school in the cloud," 114–16
    in schools, 107–8
    spending on educational, 107
    and teaching, 122–23
    use by students, 121, 122, 123,
        129–32
    use by teachers in classroom,
        119–21, 122–23
testing, province-wide, 90, 134, 221
test scores
    advantages of, 136–37
    Canadian ranking in math, 14, 15
    focus on, 134–36
    at George Webster, 21
    Ontario's emphasis on, 134–35
    and Radical Math program, 31
textbooks, 125–26
The Opposable Mind: Winning
    Through Integrative Thinking
    (Martin), 58
Thinking Schools, Learning Nation,
    225
Thomas, Gordon, 216, 217, 220–21
Thomas Tallis School, 52, 55
Thorncliffe Parents Association, 194,
    196, 197, 200

Thorncliffe Park Public School
  diversity in community, 192–93
  and sex education controversy,
    195–201
Timothy (George Webster student),
  28–29
Toronto District School Board
  child poverty in, 20
  emotional well-being survey,
    74–75
  and Infinity Lab, 109
  International Baccalaureate pro-
    grams in, 151
  and Model School for Inner
    Cities, 19
  and parents' attitudes to schooling,
    162
  and refugee sponsorship, 205
  report on specialized programs,
    145–46
  specialty schools in, 144

unions, 213–22
United Nations Educational,
  Scientific, and Cultural
  Organization (UNESCO), 16, 50
university attendance, 4, 6, 184
University of Oxford, 4

Urquart, Truly, 178, 179
U.S. National Academies of Science,
  34
U.S. National Mathematics Advisory
  Panel, 32

Valente, Lia, 129–30, 131–32, 133
Valley Park Middle School, 193, 199
Vancouver School Board, 144
Vartolas, Varinia, 108, 111–12, 113
Village on a Diet (TV show), 137
Virk, Reena, 96

Walmsley, Colin, 4–6, 7
Warner, Aaron, 46, 47, 48, 49, 210–11
Warschauer, Mark, 115–16
Wesley, Dawn-Marie, 96
Western Initiative for Strengthening
  Education in Mathematics
  (WISE Math), 31
Williams, D., 202
Willms, J. Douglas, 154
Wounded Warriors, 59
Wynne, Kathleen, 192, 193, 197, 200

Yasotharan, Sakaana, 3–4, 7, 60–62, 63
Youth and Participatory Politics
  Network (YPPN), 127, 128